Myers Barnes

CLOSING STRONG

STRONG

THE
SUPER SALES
HANDBOOK

MBA
Publishing

CLOSING STRONG
The Super Sales Handbook

Published by MBA Publications
P.O. Box 50
Kitty Hawk, N.C. 27949

Printed in the United States of America

  3 4 5 6 7 8 9

Library of Congress Catalog Number: 96-95311
ISBN: 0-9654858-1-1

Cover and page design by One-On-One Book Production, West Hills, California

"This book is a virtual up-to-date encyclopedia on closing the sale and turning objections into sales."
—Tony Alessandra, author of *The Platinum Rule*

"Anybody who wants to be a great salesperson must learn the science of selling. Closing Strong *presents excellent material to begin mastery of the science."*
—Jeffrey Gittomer, author of *Sales Moves* and *The Sales Bible*

"Closing Strong the Super Sales Handbook lives up to its name. This book gives the step-by-step approaches to selling, and I believe this book would benefit anyone from the beginning salesperson to the seasoned professional. This sales book is easy to read, understand, and it is filled with usable, valuable information that can make anyone improve his or her sales. It's a must read for serious salespeople."
—Lee Milteer, author of *Success Is An Inside Job*

"This is a very helpful book for anyone who wants to excel as a salesperson in today's changing marketplace. Highly recommended."
—Nido Qubein, Chairman, Creative Services, Inc.

"It is a concise, to the point compilation of the best closing methods known to man. It is the perfect handbook for the sales professional, or for that matter, anyone who wants to reach their ultimate potential in sales. All one has to do is read it, remember it, refer to it, then read it again!"
—Dr. John E. Fullagar, CEO, Career Technologies, nationally known consultant on Human Resource Evaluations

"Buy it! Read it! Live it! Closing Strong *is a book you will live by as you learn to succeed by selling. Must reading for winners...your sales will soar!*
—Art Fettig, author of *Selling Lucky* and *The Platinum Rule*

Table of Contents

Preface

My story is about how I went from a laborer (just barely "making ends meet") to my current position of helping others realize their potential by mastering the art of professional selling.

In 1989, prior to beginning my career in the sales industry, I was the owner of a business I was not particularly fond of and had achieved only a modicum of success. It was a small concrete construction company. Though I was the company principal, I also worked as a physical laborer in the business and had an annual income of less than $25,000. I was living on the Outer Banks of North Carolina, a vacation destination (or so it seemed) where all my peers were making fortunes selling real estate.

I decided a change was in order. I sold my business and moved north to Williamsburg, Virginia to receive my rightful share of the financial rewards of a career in vacation ownership sales.

Naive, as most new salespeople are about what it takes to succeed, I was certain I would do well. My friends and family have always assured me I had the "gift of gab," so I knew I could capture a prospect's interest. This new career would be a simple undertaking. I would meet new people, describe the offering, and at the end of our conversation, my prospect would give me a check.

It soon became clear this was not a real picture of how a

professional salesperson earns an income. Following several months of failure, my project director suggested that I either go elsewhere to "spin my wheels" or consider another career change.

Having invested all the proceeds from the sale of my concrete company to relocate, I was financially insolvent, emotionally drained, and bereft of any other job opportunities.

In my desperation, I convinced my employer to allow me another 15 days to prove my worth to the company, and especially to myself.

I immediately did what any beginning salesperson would do in this situation. I begged and pleaded with every family member. Finally, my mother, my sister, and an aunt all became proud owners of interval vacation homes.

I was a hero in my own eyes. Now I was certain my position was secure. Unfortunately, my employer was not as impressed. In his eyes, sales to family members were not a barometer of one's selling ability; I would have to prove myself in the arena of real life in the marketplace. I was granted another 15-day "stay," my last opportunity to convert a prospect to a customer.

Once again I felt desperate. I went to our company lounge to collect my thoughts and, by chance picked up a magazine and read an article on sales that looked interesting. Fortunately, that article provided me with the first best advice I ever received. It suggested a simple solution to achieving success in sales: Seek counsel from the number one sales person in your company. Find out what he or she is doing to achieve success, and simply do the same.

I decided to approach Mary, a tremendously successful lady in our company. She epitomized success in the vacation ownership industry. She was not only number one in the company, but one of the top salespeople in the country in her professional niche.

I presented Mary with the article and explained my dilemma. I was broke, about to be fired and was seeking advice. Would she share the secret of her success with me?

Her response is etched in my memory. "Myers, I am fortunate that I live quite a distance from work and have a lot of driving time." Totally bewildered, I asked "What does driving time have to do with success in sales?" At that moment, Mary produced an audio cassette series by Zig Ziglar, explaining that she listened to tapes en route to work each morning to educate herself in sales techniques.

I was amazed. It was a revelation to me that there were books and tapes that actually teach people how to sell! I was never a model student, so the concept of learning sales techniques from these was totally novel to me.

"Could I borrow your books and tapes?" I asked. To my surprise, I experienced what salespeople fear the most. . . rejection. Mary refused to lend me her materials. She softened the blow by suggesting that my borrowing her tapes would not have the same result as my purchasing the tapes. If I were to buy the tapes, I would listen with more concentration and conviction. She did, however, give me a catalog of audio and video selections.

I had the catalog, yet no idea what to purchase first. Though by title alone, *The Psychology of Selling* and *Twenty Four Closing Techniques* seemed like good places to begin.

So, I had what seemed to be the answer, yet one major obstacle existed—finances. I was about to be fired, my reserves were exhausted, and the thought of investing $120 was overwhelming. But I was committed, not so much to success, but to not limping back to my hometown and admitting to friends and family that I had failed.

I placed the order and had the two tapes shipped express. Mary was right; the fact that I had invested my own money prompted my intense study. For the next 15 days, I rose one hour earlier than usual, watched the video *Twenty Four Closing Techniques,* and in the evening, watched it again. Between appointments during the day I devoured the audio series *Psychology of Selling.* I thought and lived the two-tape series. I was rewarded with a sale in that 15-day period. During the following 15 days, I invested every available free hour to the tapes and within 30 days had earned $10,000 in commissions. I had earned in 30 days what would have taken me six months to earn in my concrete-pouring job.

This marked a new beginning for me. Since then, I have studied sales and marketing techniques, as well as new avenues for personal development, never less than 30 minutes a day and sometimes as much as 8 to 10 hours daily. Overall, I have benefited by devoting thousands of hours to studying books and tapes and to attending valuable seminars. All these sources of information and encouragement have meant the difference between success and failure in my life. Thank you Mary.

I am a perennial student of sales and personal development training and a firm believer that selling is a learned and practiced skill. Anyone committed to seeking the knowledge, committed to studying the techniques, and most importantly committed to taking the necessary training to perfect his or her skills is capable of an immeasurable degree of success.

What is offered in the following pages will propel you to success. It has made an incredible difference in the careers of multitudes of other salespeople. It will do the same for you, guaranteed. So strap yourself in. Hold tight and get ready for the ride you've been waiting for—it's all within the following pages.

Let's get going!

Introduction

There are techniques to closing a sale. Yet some sales-training professionals, and salespeople are saying to learn specific closing techniques is to conform to an obsolete era of the sales profession. It has even been suggested that closing techniques are nothing more than manipulation.

If you create a fabulous presentation with a good script designed to close the sale, you are not seeking a relationship but merely a one night stand. It seems some people believe if you make enough calls and deliver an excellent presentation, the sale will almost occur by itself. To put it mildly, this simply is not true.

Granted, we are closing differently today than in the 60s, 70s and 80s, but there are fundamentals that have always worked, and continue to work, creating great success in a salesperson's career. Closing is *the* fundamental element of success in sales.

Relationship selling, partnering and consultive selling are the valid, modern day selling strategies. However, they certainly are not meant as a replacement for the time-honored skill of closing. Some products call for salespeople to operate on the premise of the one-time call and close. Others may require spending months or years working with a client to determine needs, build trust and credibility before closing the transaction. Regardless, it still comes down to gaining commitment and reaching the final agreement, which is closing the sale.

You can spend a lot of time with a prospect, but in the end, if you do not close, you do not get paid. Closing is not an event that will occur on its own. Even if you have a phenomenal relationship with a prospect, you must be prepared to ask for the order. You cannot delude yourself into believing an excellent presentation or numerous calls will entice potential customers to automatically agree, fill out your contracts and write the check.

Elements of a Sale

There are, in my estimation, six critical steps to a sale:

1) prospecting

2) qualifying

3) presenting or demonstrating

4) overcoming objections

5) closing the sale

6) following up and following through.

Yet, if you carefully analyze each of the critical steps, you will acknowledge each requires specific closing techniques and skills.

When Vince Lombardi assumed the position of Head Coach for the Green Bay Packers, he was asked his strategy to turn around and lead the struggling team to its eventual number-one position.

Mr. Lombardi said, " I plan to lead by becoming 'brilliant at the basics.'" The basics being passing, running and kicking the ball. Critics and skeptics alike challenged and continued to query this strategy. Nevertheless, Vince Lombardi never lost focus on the basics of the game—running, passing and kicking.

Let us, as professional salespeople, maintain focus on the basics of selling. Closing skills are the basics. Closing is the foundation of all the great sales champions. Products and services require someone to sell them. You will urge your customer forward when you are prepared to ask for the order, that is, close the sale.

Sales as a Profession

Selling is a tough business. It is a profession with an endless series of pitfalls, most of which are emotional. As salespeople we ride the emotional roller coaster which is fueled by fear of rejection and failure and the highs of encouragement and success.

You must continuously deal with the reality that all your efforts and energies hinge on the approval of others. Our job, therefore, is to gain commitment and approval. But, whenever we are dependent on others for our security, there is a degree of frustration we will naturally experience.

I am often asked, "How do you stop experiencing the rejection and frustration of selling?" I respond by honestly explaining that you do not stop experiencing rejection and frustration; it's just a natural part of the profession of sales.

You must accept that professional selling is extremely challenging. And because of the challenges it renders, it also provides unimaginable and unlimited opportunities. Selling is an incredible profession affording you the possibility to earn what 95 percent of the world considers a dream or fantasy.

Your potential earnings in the sales profession are annual incomes of six and seven figures. Five percent of the self-made millionaires in America are excellent salespersons, so financial independence in sales is not just a wish or a dream, but a reality.

Many years ago, a friend pointed out that professional selling is one of six careers available in this country in which you can actually achieve your dreams and fulfill your aspirations. My friend Bill cited five other careers where it's possible to earn immeasurable incomes and experience great success: professional athlete, business owner, physician and attorney, president or CEO of a company, entertainer.

Professional athlete: At my height, weight and age, the probability of excelling as an athlete is slim. However in sales, unlike sports, your genetics, physical attributes or age do not determine the magnitude of your achievements. In fact, sales is the most non-discriminating profession available. You can be African American, Caucasian, Asian, short, tall, beautiful or plain.

Entrepreneurship: As business owner, you can amass great wealth, but there are risks involved. You need money to start the business, good cash flow and effective management. As Peter Drucker related, "You are only in business as long as your can afford your mistakes." Aside from our clothes and our cars our capital expenditure, as salespeople, is small compared to the business owner.

Physicians and attorneys: Many physicians and lawyers through years of education and hard work have accumulated fortunes. In my case, as well as Bill's, we lacked the educational requirements to become lawyers and doctors, yet Bill as a salesman, had consistently earned a six-figure income for years which had established his financial independence.

President or CEO of a major corporation or a fortune 500 company: Many wealthy people have led large organizations to prominence and were richly rewarded with huge compensation plans and stock options. But now the rules of businesses are changing. With the old business agreement you gave the company loyalty and you, in turn, received security. Today the new business deal does not offer retirement or even a gold watch. Company security and long-term careers are becoming a thing of the past because of business relocation, overseas competitiveness and downsizing. Today, you can also be fired at the first signs of a loss of profits. However, a career in sales promises lifetime security, and as a skilled salesperson you don't answer to anyone but yourself.

Celebrated entertainer: People can become great actors or musicians, but it takes more than perseverance, it also requires a lot of luck which usually means knowing the right people. A career in sales is much easier. Success waits for any individual willing to pay the price and overcome the challenges.

Though selling is a tough profession so are all the other professions mentioned. The fields are very demanding and as difficult as a sales career, that's why the rewards are so high. After all, if any of these professions were easy, they would be filled by unskilled amateurs unwilling to pay the price. Earnings, too, would only be average.

Closing as a Skill

So what's the cure for the tough times, those periods when you experience the emotional roller coasters and challenges of selling? The remedy is motivation.

But how do you stay motivated? You've been to the seminar, listened to the tapes, read the warm and fuzzy feel-good books, but the moment the world and its real challenges hit you head on, your motivation diminishes or completely disappears. That, my friend, is because the motivation you have received in the past was outward motivation and designed as a temporary fix. Outward motivation is the rah-rah bouncing-around-expression of feelings. True motivation is a result of an enhanced feeling of competency. Competency comes from having skills and being excellent at what you do. Closing-the-sale skills provide you with the competency to be excellent, the best in your field.

Closing, like any skill, can be learned, mastered and internalized. When you finally apply the skills, your competency will increase. Increased competency leads to greater results and more production, and whenever you are producing results you are internally, permanently motivated.

Whether you're a seasoned professional or just starting a sales career, understand there is no such thing as a natural-born salesperson. Rest assured, as the doctor delivered you at birth, she did not exclaim, "Now here's a natural-born closer!" Nor did the doctor make predictions to the parents of the Olympic athlete or musician. Both the athlete and entertainer achieve greatness by mastering their skills through practice, repetition and application, as you will when you apply the methods and techniques of this book.

What Is Closing?

According to Webster's dictionary, closure is to bring finality. . . finish. . .completion.

With this definition in mind, **"Closing is the natural ending to a great presentation."** Earlier I mentioned certain critical steps involved in the completion of a sale:

1) prospecting

2) qualification

3) presentation

4) overcoming objections

5) closing the sale and

6) follow through.

Closing is actually the final step. It's the natural ending, the completion of the sales process.

Let me illustrate with an event we can all relate to. Suppose you were to attend a music concert. The stage was perfect. The performance was outstanding. As the program concludes, what is the natural ending to the musical concert? Applause. As applause is the natural ending to the musical presentation, so is closing the natural ending to your sales presentation.

Analyze the process. First, you prospect for a qualified business or individual. By the way, in most cases you must realize prospecting and qualifying are events that are occurring simultaneously. After all, the function of prospecting is to obtain a qualified lead so you can deliver your presentation or demonstration.

So you have prospected and qualified. Now you deliver your presentation. At some point during the presentation your prospect will offer objections. Your next step is to overcome the objections. After overcoming the objections, the final step in the sales process is to close.

Depending on your offer, you may be involved in a one-call closing situation. Lower-priced intangible items, door-to-door sales, timeshares, health club memberships and various other products and services tend to lean toward the one-call close. If you are involved in the one-call selling situation you must close skillfully, without hesitation, with the realization you will never have an opportunity again to conclude the transaction.

Suppose your product or service requires multiple calls. You may represent real estate, business products, medical sales, or expensive tangible goods or services. Though you may not close (conclude the transaction) on the first visit, closing skills are still essential. Why? Because if you are not going to close the sale at this time, you still need a commitment to see your prospect again. What is commitment in multiple-sales calls? Perhaps it is another appointment at a specific time and date. Or the commitment could be that the next meeting would require all decision makers to be present. Commitment could be as simple as clarifying there is a need and a budget allocated to obtain your offering.

Regardless, one-call closing where the final transaction is completed on the first visit, or multiple-call selling, where the close is obtained by progressive commitments until the transaction is concluded, closing will always be the natural ending to the sales process.

2

The Sale
Before the Sale

Enthusiasm and Confident Expectations

What You Need to Know and Have Before You Sell

W hy do people buy? When I ask this to both individuals and audiences, I usually get these logical answers:

1.   **It was the right price:** If a customer really desires the product or service, cost is not a factor.

2.   **It's what I need:** People seldom buy what they need! In most cases, desire drives the customer to spend beyond his basic needs to purchase what he wants.

3. **It's what I can afford:** In this country many of us tend to spend more than we earn, to the point of often living above our means.(Generally, our society is not recognized for its ability to save money.)

Your customer buys many products like real estate, furniture, cars, or computer systems for emotional reasons and then justifies the purchase logically. Prices, terms and even quality are the logical explanations, and salespeople and consumers alike believe we become involved because of these. But the truth is, consumers rarely make a purchase based on logic.

We are emotional beings and every choice in life is flushed through emotional levels prior to reaching logical channels. We become excited first and then we rationalize our decision to buy something by saying, "It was the right price or it was what I needed."

In truth your customer never "buys" a product or service. He buys the feeling or perception of satisfaction that your product or service will provide. It is not just a commodity, but a dream fulfillment. Your customer will see himself benefitting in some way by possessing what you have to offer.

Because buying decisions are usually based on emotions, here are the keys to selling:

Enthusiasm

You have heard it before, and I will stress it again. Your degree of enthusiasm, your excitement about your product, your career, your company, and a high level of self-confidence will always account for your success in closing the sale. Since buying decisions begin at an emotional level, a sale only occurs when there is a transfer of your enthusiasm to the customer.

Look at the last four letters of enthusiasm. IASM means *I Am Sold Myself*. Until you become excited nothing will happen. Your customer is unable to become emotionally involved until you deliver your presentation with a white-hot excitement that spurs your prospect's interest. To be able to convince your prospect, you must go beyond simply knowing your product to truly believing in and loving the worthwhile benefits and solutions your product or service satisfies.

Henry Ford attributed his success to his enthusiasm. He believed that enthusiasm is the most valuable quality a human being can possess. His famous motto, displayed over his fireplace, said:

Enthusiasm

"You can do anything if you have enthusiasm. Enthusiasm is the yeast that makes your hope rise to the stars. Enthusiasm is the sparkle in your eye, it is the swing in your gait, the grip of your hand, the irresistible surge of your will and your energy to execute your ideas. Enthusiasts are fighters. They have fortitude. They have staying qualities. Enthusiasm is at the bottom of all progress! With it there is accomplishment. Without it there are only alibis."

Once while I was giving a seminar, an attendee told me she lacked enthusiasm. There were credibility issues surrounding the products and the company she worked for, and to complicate matters she was disenchanted with the sales profession.

My advice to Linda was the same as I have given to countless others. That is, if you do not believe in your company, product or profession, or if you wouldn't use the product yourself or recommend it to your best friend, then you are involved with the wrong product, service or possibly, profession. When this is the case, I always recommend the person make a change. Otherwise, the individual will never develop the enthusiasm needed to succeed.

Remember, a sale is a transfer of enthusiasm. In your mind picture a cup. Mentally pour your enthusiasm into this cup until it is full. Now picture your prospect possessing an empty cup prior to your meeting. Since a sale is a transfer of enthusiasm, you must pour the contents of your cup into his. You can only give the exact amount of enthusiasm that you have to your prospect.

Confident Expectations

The next key quality all top-closing professionals possess is the expectation that a potential customer will say yes if asked often and at the right times.

During a corporate training session for a real estate division of a Fortune 500 company, Guy, a top producer for the organization asked, "Myers, does this mean you believe we can actually will a customer into ownership?"

I answered: "Guy, suppose you were in your car driving to an appointment. For 30 minutes prior to your appointment you verbally repeated affirmations such as, "I'm happy to serve and my prospect excitedly awaits my product and service." All the while you visualize the successful completion of the meeting—closing the sale.

Now let's observe another scenario. This time you're driving to your meeting. You affirm mentally and out loud, "This appointment will not go well. They probably won't own today. I'll drop off my brochures, be on my way, and maybe they will call me back later."

Directing the question from Guy to the group, I asked which of the two mental and verbal rehearsals prior to the appointment would enhance the probability of a sale.

In unison the group responded that the probabilities would be enhanced by rehearsing the positive affirmations and visualizations verses the negative ones.

Again, quoting Henry Ford, "If you think you can, or think you can't, you are right."

You see, driving to the appointment with the expectancy of a positive outcome does not guarantee a sale; however, it certainly increases the probability. So, expectations with a confident, positive attitude may not insure the sale, but you may be certain if you take the second approach and visualize a negative outcome, this prospect will not buy. "I'll just drop off the brochures," will almost guarantee no sale.

Often, when conferring with salespeople prior to their appointments, we formulate a pre-call strategy. The first question always is, "What is it your prospect would like to own," or "What do you plan on helping them acquire?" Usually we receive a reply such as, "Well

I don't think they are ready to own yet; they will not act today. I'm just giving information at this time."

Do you understand what occurs with this type of mind set? The salesperson's expectation mentally predisposes himself to the outcome he expects, which is for the sale not to occur.

So when does a sale occur? It occurs first in your mind before your sales call. The person who first must be sold on ownership is you. I call this the "sale before the sale." Therefore, you must believe in advance that when you ask your prospect to say yes, he will say yes.

✦ First, your enthusiasm must be transferred to the prospect,

then

✦ It is your confident expectations that will cause you to act boldly and ask for the order.

3

Controlling Closing Fears

W e have discussed the positive elements needed to conclude the sale—enthusiasm and confident expectations. Now, it's appropriate to examine the fear the prospect often feels when we attempt to close the sale.

Earlier we defined closing as the natural end to a great presentation. Yet, for the average salesperson, closing can be the most tormenting part of the sales process. It can make us reluctant, anxious and very tense. Also, closing can be the time when the customer experiences the same emotions of reluctance and anxiousness. Remember the process of transferring our enthusiasm to the prospect? We exchange our negative emotions the same way; and these feelings will help block the sale.

When the prospect experiences tension and negative emotions at the moment of closing, this is known as "buyer's remorse in advance." She can experience this even if you have transferred 100 percent enthusiasm and confident expectations. Whenever your prospect reaches the point where the decision to own must be made, whenever she must decide between a yes or no, and she is not 100 percent certain she wants the product, she will experience her greatest fear, and that fear is the fear of failure. The prospect's fear of failure equals the fear of making a mistake. We have all made buying mistakes such as purchasing a product that did not meet our expectations. Or maybe later we felt we paid too much, and so on.

When "buyer's remorse in advance" overwhelms the prospect at the moment of closing, she begins to procrastinate and vacillate rather than commit and make the decision to proceed forward. She says statements such as, *I need to think it over, I'll get back with you later,* or *I need to discuss this with my accountant, attorney or take it before the committee.* What the prospect is truly saying to you is *I'm experiencing buyer's remorse and am afraid of making a decision.*

The prospect's fears are often enough to prohibit the sale, but there is also the salesperson's fear of rejection and hearing the word "No" at the moment of closing. Because of this fear, closing, for the average salesperson, can be the most tormenting part of the sales process.

Why is it we fear rejection and the word "no"? Psychologists tell us our fear of rejection and the word "no" stems from our childhood. As a baby we enter into the world without fears or preconceived notions. Our fears are taught to us. Mainly, we learn our fears from our parents through unintentional destructive criticism.

Ever hear the phrase "terrible two's?" It is at this stage of life we learn to walk. We are enormously curious, have no fear and want to explore everything. If not stopped by the watchful parent, a child could easily hurt and even kill himself.

So how do parents teach and train their children? By saying the word "no." By the time children are past their second birthday, they will have heard the word "no" thousands of times. ("No, don't do it." "I said no." "No, put that down." "Stop it," etc.) Often a parent will have reinforced "no" with a little pain, such as a slap on the hand or pop on the bottom side. Findings conclude that by the time the average person reaches adulthood, he or she will have experienced the word "no" somewhere between 116,000 and 148,000 times. Is it any wonder we fear rejection and the word "no"?

The salesperson will benefit by understanding that the word "no" you hear, is nothing more than a knee-jerk reaction from your prospect. Since we are taught our fears through the word "no," "no" is just the natural response you will get at the moment of closing when your prospect is experiencing buyer's remorse in advance. The fear of failure, or making a mistake, literally drives the potential customer to retreat to her safest response, which is to say "no."

Here's an example of what salespeople experience daily. A person walks into an automobile showroom, looking for a new car. The salesperson approaches and says, "May I help you"? Automatic response, "No thanks, I'm just looking." You hear that response most often in retail stores. A perspective buyer walks into the establishment, literally on a mission to purchase, and the salesperson approaches with, "May I help you?" The knee-jerk reaction, the natural response she usually hears is "No, I'm just looking."

Whenever a prospect is in a position to buy but is experiencing the possibility of a mistake, he will protect himself with the "no" response.

By the way, if you as a salesperson fear the word "no," you have placed yourself in a profession where rejection is imminent! Even if you are a top salesperson representing popular top-of-the-line products, as many as four out of five of those you call on will say "no." When the economy is down and competition is keen, you may experience "no" as much as 90 to 95 percent of the time.

Be aware you will hear "no" many times. The top pro expects it, prepares for it and is able to continue forward by possessing sound closing techniques and skills.

The final point about rejection is you cannot take it personally. Realize when people say "no" to you they are just offering the automatic response. They are not rejecting you as a person. They are saying "no" to the price, terms, product, delivery schedules or the situations and circumstances surrounding your offering, but not to you personally.

Conquering Your Closing Fears

The cure for rejection is simple.

◆ **Don't take rejection personally:** Now that you understand the prospect's fear of failure, keep in mind your prospect is not rejecting you.

✦ **Expect rejection:** This doesn't mean to be negative. It doesn't contradict the need for confident expectations. Just realize that usually a sales call will end with the prospect's refusal or semi-refusal. What is a semi-refusal? When you are offered objections such as, "I need to think about it," "I'll get back to you later," "I need to discuss this with someone else," and so on.

On the average, more than 80 percent of all sales take place after the salesperson makes five to seven closing attempts. In other words, you must ask the prospect to own your product or service, at minimum, five to seven times before he buys. What's surprising is that 50 percent of all sales calls end without the salesperson attempting to close even once.

This means you should expect and anticipate the prospect to say "no" or to offer a semi-refusal at least five to seven times before he says yes. By anticipating the possibility of refusal, you are able to plan your closing.

✦ **Script, memorize and rehearse the closing techniques:** You learn to close by having a planned technique. All closes are scripted, memorized, then adapted to the individual situation.

The average salesperson closes poorly because he does not take the time to learn the techniques. And he lacks the ability and skill to ask for the sale the five to seven times without giving up.

We have all heard the term "art and science." Closing is a very specific art and science. Yet, you must understand you can never practice the art without first mastering the science. Memorization of the technique is the science. After you memorize and internalize word for word, you practice the art.

Consider a professional actress, for instance. On screen her performance appears effortless. But, what is unseen is the scripting and practice that occurs prior to the performance. First she must memorize her script word for word. Then, only after mastering the "science," the script, is she able to perform.

Remember, closing is a skill, and with any skill such as acting, riding a bicycle or playing a musical instrument, it can be mastered by practice and rehearsal. As you commit the techniques to memory, you free your mind to appropriately respond to your prospect's questions and objections.

✦ **Confront your fears:** Ralph Waldo Emerson said: "Do what you fear most and the death of fear is certain." For many, asking for the order once, much less the average five to seven times, creates insurmountable fear. Yet, your obstacles to closing will melt away, if instead of trembling, you boldly approach your prospect.

Expect to feel uncomfortable as you first develop your skills. It's natural to feel uneasy doing something you have not mastered. Through experience you will gain the strength, courage and confidence to face your fear, and it will fall aside when you make up your mind to take action—ask for the order and close the sale.

Overcoming Buying Fears

Usually, indecision and procrastination on the part of the prospect will follow your closing. If your prospect is indecisive or wishes to put off the decision to own, then you have not eliminated his fears. Beyond the fear of making a mistake, by buying your product or service, the prospect may also be afraid of the words you speak.

We communicate our presentation by words. Your words paint a picture of your product or service. The words you use will either multiply a prospect's fears or evoke his confidence. Negative words will generate negative thoughts, while positive words will generate positive thoughts.

Listed on the left are the negative words which breed fear and skepticism. The words in the column on the right evoke confidence.

Don't Say	Instead Say
Agent: Agent is threatening and provokes a negative thought.	**Representative or Consultant:** To consult is to offer helpful advice and render service.
Buy: To buy is to give up security, which is money.	**Own, acquire, get involved:** People love to own. They don't like to buy.
Cheaper: Diminishes value.	**Less expensive, more affordable:** Reflects smart value consciousness.
Commission: They do not like to pay your commission as part of the purchase price. They expect us to negotiate our commission.	**Fee for service:** Your service always outweighs the fee.

Contracts: Sounds stiff, formal, difficult and requires the service of an attorney before signing.

Paperwork, agreement: Connotation of mutual understanding.

Problem: Everyone has enough problems. Don't complicate the sale.

Challenge or situation: We rise to the call of a challenge.

Cost or price: It always costs to much and the price is too high.

Total value: Equates with a fair return for the investment.

Deal: "Make a deal" or "Get a deal," sounds shifty. May be too good to be true.

Value or opportunity: An investment that leads to a favorable end.

Down payment: A request for security (money). Indicates future payments.

Initial investment: The beginning of a positive result.

Monthly payment: People fear incurring more debt and already have enough payments.

Monthly investment: Money toward value and profit.

Pitch: Carnival conman, carpet bagger.

Presentation: Introduce an opportunity.

Sell or sold: People do not want to be sold to and do not want you selling to them.

Help them to own or acquire, Get them involved: Mr. Smith, once involved as an owner, you will enjoy the benefits.

Sign: Never sign anything until checking with the attorney.

Approve, OK, authorize, endorse: Mr. Smith, could you OK the agreements, plus authorize the paperwork, approve the order, please.

Standard: Implies commonness, blandness, the everyday.

Included features: Positions the ordinary to the extraordinary.

Ups, be backs: These words are industry slang. Let your customer hear, "Sam you're up," or "Jenny, your 'be backs' are here," and you will send them running out the door.

Customer, Prospect: Our business is the customer—to whom we owe our success.

Picture the following closing situation. A poor salesperson asks for the order: "Mr. and Mrs. Walker, it really doesn't cost that much. This model is only twenty-four thousand dollars. The down payment is eight grand and the monthly payment is five-hundred fourteen dollars and twelve cents. The only thing I need you to do is sign the contracts, and we'll get the ball rolling. It's a good deal, isn't it?"

The wise salesperson, always a professional communicator, asks for the same order in a non-threatening manner: "Mr. and Mrs. Walker, the total investment is only twenty-four thousand. That would require an initial investment of eight thousand with a monthly investment of only five hundred fourteen dollars. Wouldn't you would agree it's a wise investment for your family, as well as a tremendous value? Mr. and Mrs. Walker, all that's necessary to begin the process is for you to authorize the agreements."

The first scenario creates visions of the salesperson we want to avoid. The second scenario involves a non-threatening salesperson and is more likely to build the confidence of the prospect, whereby he becomes a customer.

◆ **Occasions for Negative Words:** There is a moment when you are allowed the use of negative words, and that is when you are being compared to your competition. (The rule is never knock the competition. Every negative statement you make about your competitor's product or service just makes you look bad.)

When you are being compared to your competitor you can help yourself by mentioning they have deals, while you offer value and opportunities. "In fact, Sam Smith is a good agent and his prices are cheap, but allow me to share with you the benefits and features which will be included with your investment."

Commit the above power words to your vocabulary and use them as a natural non-threatening way to present your offer and close the sale. In your presentation, your choice of words will help spawn a positive response.

4

The Prerequisites of Closing

Before you attempt to close, you must earn the right to close. Prior to asking for the order, there are essential conditions that must exist. Any attempt to conclude the sales process without meeting these essential conditions will not only result in a lost sale but could be misconstrued as high-pressure selling tactics.

1. The Customer Must Want or Need Your Product or Service

Your obligation in professional selling is to provide solutions to meet the customer's requirements. If a need for your product or service does not genuinely exist, or if it is clear to you that what you have to offer will not satisfy the prospects' problems with solutions that are in their best interest, then move on to other prospects.

Secondly, in regards to wanting what you have to offer, prior to asking for the order you must have kindled a strong buying desire. Awakening the buying desire is the function of the presentation. Also, the function of the presentation is to bring clarity and understanding about the benefits of your products and services. If you prematurely attempt to close before arousing sufficient buying desire or before your prospects gain complete understanding of the benefits, you will destroy your chance for the sale.

2. Your Customer Must Be Able to Use Your Product or Service

Your customer should be able to take advantage of your offering for its intended use. This means never oversell or undersell. Selling a small, low-volume copy machine to a medium-sized business is underselling their needs. Likewise, placing a high-speed copier capable of producing 20,000 copies per month to a two-person start-up venture is grossly overselling the small business.

In the following chapters you will discover in depth, the qualification process so as to be sure your customer will be able to take maximum advantage of what you are offering.

3. The Customer Must Be Able to Afford Your Product or Service

Your customer should not only have sufficient funds to buy, but be able to own without being strapped. If individuals and companies are sold products that result in a financial burden, they are not truly enjoyed.

Whenever my wife and I enjoy dinner out, she invariably seeks the waiter's recommendation. It's not that she lacks confidence in her ability to select a meal, only that she seeks reassurance.

In most cases your customer seeks your recommendation prior to the buying decision. Like my wife, it's not that the buyer lacks total self-confidence with his decision, only that he seeks reassurance. As a salesperson, you operate as an assistant buyer and many times will be asked, " In your opinion what do you recommend?" And you answer, "This particular model would be the best one for you." The customer then places the order based on your advice.

Therefore, be sensitive and only offer perfect solutions that satisfy the customer's wants, needs and budget.

Common Selling Errors

Failure to ask for the order: The main reason people do not buy is they are not asked to own. As we discussed earlier, up to 50 percent of all sales calls end without the salesperson attempting to close even once.

Even when you do attempt to close, statistics indicate the average sale does not occur until the prospect is asked to own a minimum of five to seven times. In my estimation, five to seven attempts are conservative, and I suggest you that must ask an even greater number of times using multiple closing techniques.

Only a small percentage of salespeople possess the technical ability to ask for the order multiple times. The average not-so-successful salesperson waits until the end of the presentation, then nervously shifts back and forth, asking for the order in the following manner: "Is this what you had in mind?" or the classic, "Well, what do you think?" By the way, when you ask people what they think, you're giving them a feeling you are indecisive and their response will be, "I want to think about it."

You must be eager, prepared and confident to close. And the more ways you know how to ask, the more likely you are to ask, thus the more likely you are to close.

Prejudging

Carry this statement throughout your selling career: "Prejudging is not prequalifying." Most salespeople try to determine the customer's ability and willingness to own by prejudging. Prejudging usually occurs during the initial moments of the meeting. The salesperson may judge the customer by his appearance, car or job.

One day, during a sales meeting, Steve, a top producer, substantiated this tendency of salespeople. His father, a successful surgeon, never reveals his profession when shopping for high ticket merchandise such as luxury automobiles and real estate investments. He also intentionally dresses down and drives in his older car to appear less than qualified. Steve's father has been able to shop unattended and almost inconspicuously. If he drove his Jaguar and dressed in his professional attire, he most likely, would have received a lot of attention.

It is human nature that makes our first impressions our lasting impressions, but you must resist human nature and not judge people on the surface. Ability and willingness to own are not determined by outward appearances.

(Regarding our nature to prejudge during the first few moments of the initial contact, remember, the prospect will also prejudge you. So it is important that you portray a professional image of yourself, product and company.)

Let's say a salesperson hasn't prejudged by appearance and disqualified a qualified prospect. The second time prejudging may occur is somewhere during the presentation when a salesperson decides the prospect does not want to own because she asks too many questions or voices concerns or objections. The salesperson loses heart.

Remember, a sale is a transfer of emotion, and the moment you decide the prospect will not own is when your energy and enthusiasm dissipates and you deliver a poor presentation.

You will learn about objections in chapter six. You should expect them to occur and not allow negative feelings to hamper your presentation.

Talking to much: Mediocre sales organizations focus their training on product knowledge instead of sales methods. Therefore the salesperson's presentation centers around product knowledge and a lot of facts. Poor salespeople talk too much and want to tell everything. The prospect will not be dazzled with a salesperson who talks too much.

Telling is not selling. God gave you two ears and one mouth so you should listen twice as much as you talk. The excellent salesperson questions skillfully and listens attentively to the prospect's needs. She asks her way into a sale, she doesn't talk her way into it.

Talking past the close: The most valuable instruction my father gave was, "Son, when they are ready to buy, they are ready to buy...stop talking and grab your contract."

When you ask a closing question and your prospect confirms he is ready to own, the conversation stops, your presentation ceases and you start preparing the paperwork.

As an example, a salesperson asks, "Current production schedule guarantees delivery by the end of the month. Is that satisfactory?" The prospect answers, "Yes, it is." At that moment he has made the decision to own. End your presentation. Move swiftly to prepare the contractual agreements.

Arguing with the prospect or customer: When you receive objections or challenges to your claims and you defend your product, you are in essence telling the person he is wrong. People dislike to be told they are wrong, even if they are. You are in business to win the customer, not a battle. Always be agreeable. Remember, when people have objections, respond to their questions in a positive non-threatening way. "A man convinced against his will, is of the same opinion still."

Knocking the competition: The first rule is to not make reference to your competition. If, however, something is said about the competition, negative or positive, simply reply with, "They are a fine company, and seem to do a good job."

If you are asked why he should purchase from you verses the competition, respond with a two-part question.

Ask, "Why do you feel you should do business with that company?" Allow him to answer and he will tell you how he wants to do business. Follow-up the question with, "What would cause you not to do business with that company?" Listen carefully to hear objections why he would not do business with your competitor. This information provides you with elements upon which to build your presentation and overcome objections on what you have been told, verses your assumptions.

When to Close
How to Respond to Questions During the Close

When do you close: Donna, a new home salesperson, approached me one day after a sales meeting and said, "I'm just not sure of the exact moment, the appropriate time, to close. I've internalized and scripted my closing techniques, and I understand them. I'm just not sure of the proper moment when I should bridge to the close."

I asked, "Donna what is your favorite part of the sales process; prospecting, qualifying, presenting, overcoming objections or closing?"

"Oh Myers, I absolutely love delivering my presentation. I'm so excited about the company, and I love showing property and homes."

"Like yourself Donna, most salespeople prefer the presentation portion of the process. It is in essence a time for you to socialize. But what you are asking is, when do I stop socializing and get down to business?

"What you are doing is giving the entire presentation and

waiting for what you think is the one moment that is most appropriate to close. Donna, the close usually occurs at the end of the presentation, but it has been building all along throughout the presentation.

"It is the process of **gaining commitment.** You see, there are commitments and minor closes that must occur during the selling process before the prospect makes the major commitment to own.

"For example, you must first gain commitment to agree to an initial appointment, which includes a specific time, location and date. Donna, as insignificant as this seems, if you cannot gain the commitment and close on something as minor as the appointment, what makes you think you can close something as major as the sale?

"Suppose after obtaining the appointment you assess the needs of the prospect. Now it requires a follow-up call and the need to prepare a proposal. You still have not concluded a sales transaction, so the sale you make is the follow-up appointment. This in itself requires closing skills."

So as I further explained to Donna, you are constantly closing and gaining commitments. Commitment and minor-point closing that occur during the sales process could be as simple as determining a need and ensuring your product will satisfy a need. Selling, whether by one-call closing or through multiple-call contacts, is occurring during the entire presentation. The process of gaining commitment and closing is the presentation.

The most appropriate time to close is during a presentation and at the end of it. You don't put off asking for the order later in the day or week. After the presentation, sometimes during, the prospect usually has 100 percent of the information available and is more emotionally closer to making a decision than at any other time. Your prospect will never be closer to a decision or more emotionally involved than during or at the end of a presentation.

Recognizing Buying Signals

I'm not clairvoyant, and do not feel other sales associates are; therefore, when salespeople say they have developed a sixth-sense regarding closing, I become doubtful about that person's sales ability. I have never felt my way into a sale; and do not recommend you feel your way around to the right moment to close, possibly making the wrong assumption.

Listen attentively and carefully observe your prospects. They will tell you verbally by their words and physically by their actions when they are ready to make the decision to own. If you pay strict attention, you can almost see them waving the green flag signaling you to ask for their order.

Questions the Customer Asks Prior to Closing:

✦ **Recommendation:** We discussed this earlier. When the customer asks your opinion, he is only looking for the calm reassurance from the assistant buyer, you, as the salesperson to make a recommendation. "Mr. Smith, based on all the information you have provided, I would suggest your needs would best be met by the XYZ model. We could have this delivered and installed on the 15th of this month, or the first of the following month. Which is better for you?" The most visible verbal clue when the sale involves a couple, is when a husband and wife look at one another and ask, "Honey, what do you think?" Congratulate them on their decision to own (and move into the Handshake Close which will be discussed later). It's the same for a committee decision. Assume the sale when one partner looks at the other and asks, "What do you think?" Don't wait for the partner to say, "Let's think about it."

✦ **Features and options:** You may be questioned about features or options: "We are really interested and would like to own, but we wanted it in red."

Suggest it may be available in red. (You will be using a Take Away Close, covered in a later chapter.) Say, "Mr. and Mrs. Prospect, I'm not sure if it's readily available in red. Would you like me to check?" If one of them says yes, call or check, then say, "Good news, there is just one available, and I've placed it on hold for you while we process the paperwork." Perhaps one partner asks, "If I buy, would you include a certain option at no additional cost?" Say, "Mr. and Mrs. Prospect, I'm not sure if that's possible. However, why don't we put in writing what you would like and if it's accepted, then it's just additional value. Besides we won't know unless we ask."

✦ **Delivery:** "How soon can I get it?" is a buying question. Use this buying question to ask a closing question. The answers you get from the prospect serve two purposes. First, it confirms the prospect is serious. Second, it causes the person to tell you he's making the decision to own. "Mr. Prospect, if we proceeded forward today, we may be able to have it delivered within two weeks. Is that satisfactory?" Or you can ask, "How soon do you need it?" When the prospect questions the time frame, cease your presentation and attempt to conclude the sale.

✦ **Details:** "What about your warranty, or tell me again what comes with the offer?" Whenever the client asks you to re-explain something a second time, he is indicating he is approaching the decision to own. Utilize a "summary close"; repeat all the features and benefits, followed by an invitation to own.

✦ **Price or terms:** "Do you offer terms?" Reply with something like, "Have you prearranged financing or would you like me to handle the details?" If he says, "The price is higher than I expected," you can say, "Mr. Prospect, suppose I could offer you terms that would allow you to own on a monthly basis." Questions concerning price and terms offer the perfect opportunity to close. Be sure to answer all buying questions with a question that either confirms ownership or actually leads the prospect into ownership.

✦ **Value:** "How do I know this is the best price or do you negotiate price?" When asked this question, it is pretty clear he has reached the buying decision and decided to own.

It's time to offer assurances, move to the "Paint A Fantasy Picture Close" and wrap up the details.

"Mr. Prospect, you have received the absolute best value. Your family will enjoy weekends on the lake for years to come. By the way, will you be taking title in both your names?"

Non-Verbal Clues

Keeping in mind the adage, what you do speaks louder than what you say, carefully observe your client's body language and actions:

The customer calculates the numbers or reviews the contracts: Now, he is beyond thinking about it and is financially justifying the decision. Whenever he reaches for his calculator or asks you to determine rate of returns, the monthly investment, how much it is going to cost, it's time to close. Also, when the prospect reviews the contract, it's time to close. Say for example, "Mr. Prospect, do you have any questions before we begin the paperwork?" The prospect answers no, then you proceed with the paperwork. If he answers yes, simply ask, what would that be, and let him offer the final objection.

The customers' attitude changes: They have fought all along but suddenly they become happy. With a husband and wife as prospects, the non-verbal clue may be that they touch one another or hold hands. When prospects start to feel good about the decision to own, they sometimes begin to relax, smile, laugh or suddenly become friendlier.

The customer asks for a second showing: In real estate, for instance, the presentation includes the showing of the property. When the customer asks to go back out for another viewing, this indicates he is ready to proceed forward. In this case there is no "proper" place to complete the paperwork. Usually, upon a second view, the prospect is emotionally high, and contracts can be completed outside the office or showroom. Many contracts have been completed on car hoods, kitchen tables, restaurants and so on.

The customer's posture changes: The prospect who has been leaning back will suddenly sit up straight or lean forward. Whenever someone's physical posture changes, it usually indicates he's made a decision. Ask a closing question. "Mr. Prospect, the initial investment is $5,000 and can be secured by cash or check. What would be more convenient for you?"

Many salespeople become so involved in the presentation part of the sales process that if the prospect decides to buy during the presentation, they literally will not let him. Don't become so enthralled with the sound of your own voice that you miss the buying signals indicating the customer is ready to own.

The point is you must be able to swing into the close the moment the buyer indicates the intention to own, whether it's demonstrated by verbal or physical action. A professional closes at all appropriate times and moves swiftly when the prospect is ready to own.

5

Qualify Buyers First

Change Your Perception About Rejection

Your goal in professional selling is to determine the customer's needs, offer solutions and conclude the transaction as soon as possible. However, before you can close, it is essential to qualify all potential owners prior to the presentation.

It's tempting and easy not to take this essential step. Yet spending time with qualified prospects is the key to high sales volume. In fact, sales research claims that two-thirds of the presentations given by salespeople today are wasted on individuals and companies not qualified to purchase. Since this is the case, it's no wonder selling can be so frustrating at times.

As logical and sensible as it seems to qualify prospects, many salespeople still fail to do so. Though in all honestly, this usually results from a lack of proper sales training. Many people simply don't know how to professionally qualify a potential purchaser. So they immediately launch into their presentations, focusing on the assumed need of the customer. This stems from desperation and lack of understanding more than anything. These salespeople end up discouraged and frustrated, unable to understand why they are having a difficult time closing a fair percentage of their sales.

The fact is, you simply cannot conclude a sale with an unqualified individual or company. They must have the money, desire, or need to own, and the authority to purchase.

Consequently, your first priority should always be to align yourself with those individuals or companies qualified to make a purchase.

Here are the reasons why it is essential to qualify your buyers before committing any of your valuable time or energy.

1. **Qualifying determines wants, needs and desires:** Today's consumers feel many salespeople are insensitive and uncaring. They erroneously believe a salesperson's top priority is simply making the sale. Period. They do not feel we truly care about providing the right product for their needs.

Qualifying helps both you and the prospect. Qualification is a process of discovery. A major part of your job is to uncover the true agenda, emotional and otherwise, of the individual or company. Only when you discover there is a distinct need which can be fulfilled by your product do you take steps toward committing time and energy.

2. **Qualifying provides you with the prospect's financial status:** If there is a need which can be filled by your product, your next priority is to determine whether the prospect has adequate funds available

to take advantage of what you have to offer. If financial resources are not available, then there is no reason to waste your time or theirs.

3. Qualifying provides you with the prospect's financial parameters: You don't want to oversell or undersell the potential customer.

If you present a $1,000 solution to a $10,000 need, you will frustrate your prospect and loose the sale. If you provide a million dollar solution to a quarter million dollar need, you will frustrate the prospect and loose the sale.

You qualify based on what is affordable to the need. Only present and demonstrate solutions within the financial parameters that best meet that need.

4. Qualifying determines all parties involved in the decision: There's nothing more frustrating than to knock somebody's socks off with a dynamic presentation, have a transaction mentally and emotionally wrapped up and then find out that the sale is contingent on someone else—a committee, a partner, a parent. There is a way around this though. Simply make sure that all significant decision makers are present whenever you give your presentation. If all parties are not available for a presentation, reschedule the presentation to a time that better suits everyone's schedule.

5. Qualifying determines the time frame: It is essential that you know when the prospect is willing to take advantage of your offer. Determine whether he wants to purchase today, next week, a month or a year from now.

6. Qualifying reveals the competition: When you are qualifying, you can find out whether you are competing against others for the business. It allows you to structure your presentation with your competitor's product, services and prices in mind.

7. **Qualifying helps eliminate objections before they appear:** If you question skillfully and listen attentively, prospective purchasers will tell you everything you need to know to help them with their buying decisions. Ask the right questions, and allow the prospect the opportunity to talk about herself and her concerns, then almost invariably, she will tell you her greatest needs and concerns.

Controlling the Fear of Qualification

Even though the process of qualification is so important, most salespeople avoid it. Why?

Because the average salesperson fears the process. The salesperson doesn't want to be viewed as an intruder probing into the prospect's personal territory—wants, needs, desires, financial resources, which include ability or authority to purchase. But you cannot solve a problem or provide a solution unless you properly understand a prospective buyer's needs and financial status.

Another reason salespeople may not qualify is because they would rather take the easy way out, falsely believing that they are working with a "Class A" prospect to avoid thorough research.

The Issue of Control

If you have problems controlling the sales process and influencing your prospect positively, you probably have problems being a salesperson as well.

In every meeting of two or more persons, there is a dominant person who controls the rest of the group. This is a fact. Either you are in control of the situation and circumstances or someone else is.

You have to control in order to lead. The only way you can lead your potential customers to own what you represent is to guide them.

I am often asked: "Myers, what happens if a potential customer will not cooperate and allow me to ask qualifying questions?" (In reality this rarely happens with prospects, so don't let it become an issue.)

However, when you are not certain if a prospect will cooperate, I suggest an opening statement and question to get things rolling, like the following example.

"Mr. and Mrs. Prospect, I'm not even certain if my company is able to meet your particular needs. In order to determine if I can offer you a service at the best possible value, I will need to ask a few questions to fully understand your situation. Do you mind if I ask the questions so that we may both determine if I have a solution to offer?"

If you lead into the qualification process with simple statements and questions like these, you should be able to reduce the resistance you might receive. However, if you try very hard and still cannot obtain answers to your qualifying questions, you have an alternative. *Terminate the interview.*

Think it through. It's how you make your living to support yourself and your family. It's your profession, and how you achieve your financial goals. You do not have time to waste with individuals or companies who will not cooperate.

Get over your fear of asking questions. It's in the best interest of the customer, as well as yourself. Resolve whether a perspective customer qualifies or not. You take control of your career.

The Four Areas of Qualification

There are four basic areas of qualification you must identify before beginning a sales presentation and attempting to close the sale.

1. **WANTS, NEEDS and DESIRES:** Is there a need for your product or service? If there is not a need, can you create enough desire to produce a want that turns into a need? If you do make a solid presentation and a prospective buyer still has no need or want for your product or service, then simply cut your presentation short, exit gracefully and press on to the next opportunity.

It is important during this phase to be able to differentiate between wants and needs. By nature we always want more than we need.

Here's an example. I was representing luxury second homes in oceanfront communities. Interior homes, without an ocean view, ranged from $400,000 upward. Oceanfront homes ranged in price from $800,000 to more than a million dollars. Without fail, everyone who viewed the real estate would choose to own oceanfront properties. Yet, my sales team and I also understood, though everyone wanted oceanfront, only a few could afford this luxury. The majority of our sales were interior homes because of the affordability. Though they may want oceanfront, if what is affordable is an interior home located off the oceanfront, then the need overrides the want. This is true in any sale's offering.

I have a friend who is a very successful automobile salesperson. Mark assures me that many times his prospects find it uncomfortable when he asks about their budgets. But, it is absolutely critical that he first establish their financial parameters. Like homes, those seeking automobiles often confuse their needs with their wants. It seems everyone wants the luxury automobiles, but in most cases he must be very careful to present and demonstrate only those cars they can afford.

Why? According to Mark and countless sales professionals, once prospects make an emotional commitment to a high ticket item, then are told they cannot afford it, they become frustrated and will not be open to purchasing a less costly product. It then becomes almost impossible to regain any semblance of control, assistance or direction. This entire situation, of course, can be avoided by directing customers more realistically toward a product which falls within their budget.

That is why it's imperative that you qualify. Don't oversell or undersell your prospects. Remember, what they want may not be what they need.

2. FINANCIAL RESOURCES (Money): This is a critical area. Your prospects may want or need your product or service, but if your products are not within their financial parameters, start searching for qualified prospects.

Let's look at the category for individuals and consumer goods.

If you represent products, such as automobiles, boats, real estate, or any product that may require bank financial terms, you may need to qualify your prospect in two separate categories.

A) **Down payment or initial investment:** To borrow money, you must have money. When financial terms are offered, banks or financial institutions may require the customer to have equity. The initial investment is usually paid by check.

B) **Monthly payment or investment:** Your prospect must qualify with his ability to afford the monthly investment. With some products, such as real estate and automobiles, financial institutions may require your customer to meet specific debt ratios in proportion to an income. In other words, banks and most reputable institutions will only allow a certain amount of debt to be incurred by consumers.

What if your product or service caters to businesses or companies? It then becomes essential that you determine if there is a budget for your offering. If there isn't a budget at present, can a budget be created? If financial arrangements for companies or a business must be secured from a financial institution, the same considerations (initial investment and monthly investment) may apply.

3. **AUTHORITY:** Who will be responsible for the purchase? Authority in a buying decision is absolutely critical. Will you be able to follow up, secure and deliver your presentation to all persons who will be involved in the decision to purchase?

A) **Authority for individuals:** Never fool yourself. In the case of a couple buying a home, there are always two people involved in the decision—both the husband and wife. To secure appointments and engage in presentations and attempt to close with one and not the other is a waste of time, and will usually result in no decision or a delayed decision to own.

Often, I have been involved with partnerships, joint ventures, and syndicates that purchase investment properties as a group. In most cases, I met first with one individual who assured me he was the decision maker, representing the interest of the entire group. In the early days of my career, I was gullible and believed this was true, so I would give presentations and attempt to conclude the transaction with the one, verses the entire group. I quickly learned when a group of investors is involved, then all partners pertinent to the decision to own must be present. One of the greatest errors a salesperson can make is to believe the prospect when he is told, "I make all the decisions. Just tell me what it is you have to offer."

B) **Authority for companies and business:** Even as it is getting more difficult for businesses to assemble all of the decision makers together at once, it is still essential.

Harry who represents intangible services to large companies points out, "There are many who can decide not to own, but only a few who can decide to purchase in a corporate structure."

A word of wisdom: Beware of decision breakers. Sometimes people in lower-level positions have power to say "no." Yet, because they don't have the power to say "yes," or to purchase, they will run you ragged asking for proposals, presentations and materials. It's usually an ego issue with these people.

Don't waste your time on non-decision makers or decision breakers. Get to the decision makers, and be sure your presentations and appointments are always with the company owner, CEO, or someone in authority who will be able to move forward with the decision to purchase. No one else is worthy of your time.

How do you uncover these decision makers? Simply ask, "Are others besides you involved in the decision to own or do you have final authority?" If others are involved, be sure to schedule an appointment with all of the parties involved.

Appointments with those who must check with the committee will usually result in more appointments and delayed decisions. In many cases, it could be a negotiating strategy and an excuse for suspending decisions.

4. TIME FRAME: How urgent is the need or how soon can the appropriate person or people take advantage of your offering. The time frame is critical, it determines how and when you attempt to close the sale. Also, when you will be paid!

I once shared this area of qualification with an outstanding salesperson who sold many high ticket items. Barbara says her sales soared after she started asking simple questions such as, "How pressing is your need?" She would then say, "When do you plan to take advantage of my service?" Questions such as these allowed her to properly target her presentation and closing sequence.

Questions to Ask When Qualifying: The Right Questions

Why ask questions? Because it's the only way to get the answers you need. Telling isn't selling; it's asking questions that makes a sale.

✦ Asking questions allows you to take control of the situation. You are in control not merely by the questions you ask, but because of the answers you receive.

✦ Asking the right questions removes you from the role of salesperson and establishes you as a consultant. When you ask questions with the buyer's best interests in mind and with the hope of trying to find a solution, you reposition yourself as an advisor.

Your questions are only going to be effective by the manner in which they are asked. It's important that you ask boldly and confidently and comprehend the prospect's answer. You cannot help someone or offer assistance if you do not fully understand her present situation. To lead the prospect where she wants to be, you must first establish where she is. It is your job to properly service a client. You have the absolute right to ask for all the necessary answers: 1) wants, needs, desires, 2) financial resources, 3) authority and 4) time frame.

Once again, don't be embarrassed or timid. Ask boldly in a self-assured manner that elicits a sincere reply from your prospect. Assure her that you are seeking answers to provide a solution to her need at the best value.

Questions to Qualify Wants, Needs and Desires

1. We have many models (solutions). May I ask you a few questions to help me identify which one may be the best for you?

2. What benefits would you expect as a result of our association?

3. Could you describe the ideal outcome you would like to achieve or would expect?

4. What would you like to accomplish with this purchase?

5. If you could change anything about your present situation, what would it be?

6. What type of service do you expect?

7. Are you interested in commercial or consumer grade? (If applicable.)

8. Would you use this (product or service) at your office or home? (If applicable.)

Questions to Qualify Financial Resources

1. Mr. & Mrs. Prospect, this particular model would require an initial investment of _____, and a monthly investment of _____. Is that a comfortable investment range?

2. Do you have a budget for this or an investment range in mind?

3. If you should decide to become involved with our product, would you require any financial assistance?

4. Would this be cash, or do you plan on financing the purchase?

5. Based on what you have shared with me, it seems you do not have a budget allocated, yet you seem interested. Can a budget be created? How may I assist you with the creation of a budget?

Questions to Determine Authority

1. Mr. & Mrs. Prospect, a purchase of this nature may include the family. If you don't mind my asking, would there be others involved in the decision?

2. You mentioned there would be partners or others involved with owning the (product or service). Wouldn't it make sense to schedule a time when all parties involved with the decision to own are present?

3. Would there be anyone other than yourself involved in the decision to own?

4. Would taking advantage of our service require a committee decision, or are you solely responsible for completing the transaction?

5. Who besides yourself would be reviewing the proposal?

Questions to Determine Time Frame

1. Is this an immediate need, or are you planning to purchase later in the year?

2. When would you like to take advantage of the (offer, service or product)?

3. Suppose we were to offer the ideal solution at the perfect price, would you be in a position to proceed today?

4. Are we working within a certain timetable?

5. Ideally, if we could solve your problem, how soon before you would be taking advantage of the solution?

Qualifying is a process that will continue through the course of the entire sale. But many questions will need to be answered as you and the individual or company decide on whether or not you will enter into a business relationship. You are asking the questions in advance so as to decide whether or not to devote your time and energy on an unqualified individual or company.

Changing Your Perception About Rejection

In the beginning of this chapter, it was pointed out that experts now agree as many as two-thirds of today's sales presentations are being delivered to non-qualified buyers. With this thought in mind, here are two questions:

✦ First, now that you have discovered the four areas of qualification, could you have been guilty of previously giving presentations to non-qualified buyers?

◆ Second, can you have an abundance of appointments and be successful?

Think carefully before you reply. If you have been in sales for any period of time you have probably heard that sales is a numbers game, so the secret is to put yourself in front of enough people and a certain number will purchase.

This is not necessarily true. You can have an abundance of appointments and still not be successful, especially if your appointments are with those who are not qualified to take advantage of your offering.

What is suggested will literally change your perception about rejection, and cause you to become unbelievably excited about sales in general. As a salesperson you experience rejection, not because you fail to prospect, present or close. Rejection, in most instances, is the result of your failure to qualify.

Salespeople often create their own anxiety and discouragement by failing to qualify. Once you commit to the qualification process, you should be the one to decide whether or not to continue forward with a particular individual or company.

Most salespeople see the potential customer as the person in the driver's seat with the power to either reject or accept the salesperson and the offer. They actually view the individual or company they are working with as the rejecter; they see themselves as the rejectee.

From this day on, restructure your position and see yourself, the qualifier, as the rejecter, and your unqualified leads and prospects as the rejectees.

Turn the tables on rejection by qualifying your buyer. Customers literally have to jump through four hoops before you invest time with them. If they cannot get through any of the hoops: 1) money, 2) authority, 3) wants, needs and desires, 4) a reasonable time frame—reject them and move on to a qualified prospect. Your closing will occur almost naturally when you devote your time and energy to the right people.

Keeping Score

Here is a simple and effective system to monitor your potential customer's qualifications. Countless others have successfully utilized the system to determine the qualification of prospects.

Simply take the four areas of qualification—1) wants, needs and desires, 2) financial resources, 3) authority, 4) time frame—and place a plus or minus symbol beside each area of qualification.

1) Wants, Needs and Desires   + / -_____

2) Financial Resources   + / -_____

3) Authority   + / -_____

4) Time Frame   + / -_____

As you begin your pre-appointment by phone or by in-person presentation, simply circle the appropriate symbol. As an example, suppose you give a company a plus in categories 1, 2, and 4, but a minus in authority, because the people you talk to are not decision makers. As you follow-up, this simple method reminds you your primary goal is to make a presentation to all decision makers.

Suppose categories 2 and 3 are satisfied, but there is no clarity in categories 1 and 4. Perhaps clarity is lacking because the clients possess a strong want, but because of lack of finances, the want is not what they need. Or, maybe they do not have a need at all. Does this mean you have a disqualified lead? Not necessarily; if they have the money and you are given an appointment to make a presentation to all pertinent decision makers. Then, it's your job as a salesperson to create a want or need in a specific time frame.

Now, let's suppose categories 1, 3, and 4 are satisfied, but finances (category 2) are not available. This is easy. If there isn't a budget, or a budget cannot be created, then don't waste any time on this prospect.

Becoming a Doctor of Sales

Think of yourself as a doctor. But instead of diagnosing physical ailments, and providing healing remedies, you're looking to meet people's needs through sales solutions.

Diagnosis—ask careful questions to determine the situation. Provide a solution or a prescription based on the need or situation.

Doctors always qualify before they prescribe. Prescription before diagnosis would be malpractice. If you told the doctor you had a headache, and she said "Fine, let's do brain surgery," you know she's attempting to find a solution before she even knows the facts.

Think this through. A doctor never prescribes without a diagnosis. (And, these days, before you even see the doctor, the staff qualifies you based on your finances. They ask, "Do you have health insurance, or will you be paying by cash?")

So, a doctor qualifies patients the same way a professional salesperson qualifies prospects—by asking questions.

The doctor asks where it hurts, takes your temperature, maybe takes blood or tissue samples, and so on, before prescribing a cure.

Therefore, you know prescription before diagnosis is malpractice. Remember, as Dr. Tony Alessandra once said: "Presentation before qualification is also malpractice."

Invest 15 to possibly 30 minutes of your time qualifying up front, to eliminate wasting hours, days, or possibly months delivering presentations and attempting to close sales with those who cannot or will not purchase from you.

6

Go Ahead, Make My Day...Object!

How can a prospect's objection to your offer make your day?

You may have certain notions about the prospect. You think to yourself, "My dream customer is great! We get along well, we agree, and she recognizes my offer as the perfect solution."

Wake up from your dream. Many times, if your prospect does not object, does not challenge your product and the claims you make, she will not buy. (Refer to chapter 3 and refresh your memory with the fear of failure on the part of the buyer.)

Regardless of how dazzling and complete your presentation, the fear of making a mistake might cause your prospect to be doubtful and hesitant, and you will have to deal with her concerns before you are able to conclude the sale.

So, remember, many sales do not occur without prior objections. Be glad for the opportunities to defend your product and pricing when the prospect complains. Even if the client responds in an abrasive manner she may be telling you she is emotionally involved and interested.

Objections often mean the prospect needs more information. When she says I need to "think it over," what the prospect is saying is, "I am not yet convinced and need additional information to be certain of the decision."

If the prospect says, "I need to talk this over with my accountant, attorney or any third party," she is saying, "I'm not yet certain; I need approval and assurances."

When the prospect says, "It's too expensive or I can get it cheaper elsewhere," she wants you to prove you offer the best value. "I do not like the color," means "What other colors are there, or can you get me the color I want?" And of course, the response, "I'm not interested," during your initial contact, means she does not yet have enough information to make a buying decision.

Objections are your sign posts. This input from the prospect serves as critical path markers you must follow. They represent what must be resolved during your presentation in order to close the sale. Whatever issues the prospect challenges are the most important to her and therefore, to you. Provide the prospect with your answers and she will own.

Objections indicate interest. Rest assured, if you receive no objections, your prospect is generally not interested. Normally, if your prospect does not have the financial ability to own or has no interest, she will react to your presentation in one of two ways.

She may just sit there, unemotionally, without responding to anything you say. Or, she will comment, "Yes, it sounds great," throughout the presentation. If the prospect responds either way, you are in trouble.

So, acknowledge, generally no sale takes place without objection, and when you have an objection you should inwardly rejoice and say thank you for making my day. Your acknowledgment and decision to welcome objections enables you to overcome them and conclude the sale.

Objections Versus Conditions

There is a difference between an objection and a condition. You must understand which one you are hearing from a prospect.

An objection is nothing more than an unanswered question. Somewhere in your presentation you have either said something, or failed to address an issue which leaves a question in the prospect's mind. It is fed back to you as an objection. The good thing is it's something concrete you can address and overcome.

A condition, on the other hand, is an obstacle. Conditions are barriers or situations that prevent a prospect from buying. For instance, a prospect says, "I cannot make a decision without my partner." That's a condition you cannot get around. It's a condition that says you must deliver your presentation to all decision makers prior to moving forward with the sale. Or the prospect may not meet the financial qualifications. Perhaps he has the funds available for the initial investment but because of past credit history he cannot obtain a loan. Perhaps he can afford the monthly investment but is cash poor and cannot put adequate funds together for a year or more. In both cases, these are conditions you cannot remedy even with a brilliant presentation.

Therefore, let me offer this startling scenario. Often, you waste your time trying to conclude a sale by overcoming a condition, which means you did not pre-qualify or carefully listen to your prospect. And when you receive the condition, you go ballistic trying to overcome an obstacle that is immovable. Since conditions are a "statement of fact" regarding your prospect, it doesn't matter how good you are, how developed your skills or how great your answers, you are not going to get around a condition.

Why would you even attempt to address a condition, when all you have to do is qualify the prospect prior to beginning your presentation? If you pre-qualify before your appointment, you will never experience a condition during your presentation. The entire purpose of qualifying is to determine if there are conditions that make a sale impossible, and if there are, why waste valuable time trying to overcome a condition?

What's interesting is most prospects initially feel their objections are conditions. They think when they offer the objection, they are presenting you with an obstacle and condition of fact which prohibits them from buying. So when they say, "I can't afford it" (and you know they have the budget), you rephrase the objection in your mind to "show me how I can afford it," you can overcome the objection by offering terms. So you have taken what they thought was a condition and converted it to an answerable objection.

Remember, your job is to recognize and acknowledge two facts:

1.   If you initially pre-qualify and listen carefully to your prospect, you will never experience a condition as the reason for not closing the sale.

2.   All objections are questions and requests for more information, and if you answer them to the customer's satisfaction you will close the sale.

Objections Are Predictable

Since the dawn of the first sales call, prospects have been saying to salespeople: "I need to think it over." "It's too expensive." Or "I need to talk to my brother's niece, whose son is an accountant."

The average salesperson is generally caught off guard when he or she hears "I want to think it over." He packs up his presentation, hands the prospect a brochure, and says "I'll give you a call after you've had the time to think about it."

So what's the good news? The good news is since all objections are predictable you can plan your response in advance. Like an actor in a Broadway play, you know your lines (presentation), and you know the other lines (objections) of the other performers (prospects). I tell my people in my seminars, "We know what they are going to say in advance. Therefore, since you already know what they are going to say, your job is to know what to say back before they say it."

The "Law of Six"

In sales there is a universal axiom that sales trainer Brian Tracy calls The Law of Six. It states, "customers really have no more than six objections to owning your product or service."

You may hear what seems like countless objections to sales during your career. However, if you categorize the objections you will find they normally fall into six basic categories.

In my real estate business, our objections were 1) price, 2) competition, 3) performance (as to claims), 4) finance, 5) third-party approval and 6) legal and tax benefits. After identifying all objections we received regularly, we developed iron-clad scripted answers to them. Thus, once we armed ourselves with air-tight answers to these predictable objections, which used to block the sale, my company set new sales records. The point is, you cannot wait until you are involved in the presentation and then try to make up an answer. You must proactively prepare in advance.

Your job as a professional is to discover for yourself, or with your sales team, the six common objections you hear consistently. Once identified, it's a simple process of internalizing and memorizing potent responses. Then when the predictable objections appear, you answer easily and effortlessly and automatically move to the close.

The Customer's and Salesperson's Objections

There are the objections you receive from the prospect, and as stated previously, these objections are the easiest to overcome. However, there are also the objections the salesperson creates in his own mind as to why a customer would not own. These objections we may hold in our own minds can be by far the most destructive.

For example, there may be something about your product or service that may not make 100 percent sense to you. Perhaps you are uneasy with the price or terms your company offers. In any case, you are not convinced that your product is the best value available. Therefore, when you deliver your presentation and the final objection is price or terms, and you happen to share the same beliefs as the prospect, you are unable to overcome the objection. Thus, you loose the sale.

The cure for a prospect's objections is a pre-planned response. Now the only cure for the objection in your mind is attitude! Remember, a sale is a transfer of enthusiasm, and you have to fill your cup prior to filling the prospect's. You will have to first analyze in overcoming objections whether it is yours, his or both. If it's in your mind first, you must invest the time to change your attitude. Find out more about your product and support it 100 percent. Develop the positive mindset necessary to overcome the customer's objections.

Uncover the Unspoken Objection

Many times what prohibits the sale is the one final objection hidden by a series of small objections. Your prospect knows, too, if not consciously but subconsciously, if he gives you this not-yet-spoken objection and you answer it, he will have no choice but to move forward as an owner. So he holds back this one silent objection behind a smoke screen of minor objections to avoid the buying decision.

When you are at the point where you sense the prospect is hesitating and hiding behind a smoke-screen objection ask: "Mr. Prospect, I sense a bit of hesitancy. Do you mind my asking what it is?" If you remain silent the prospect will offer an answer. Regardless of the answer, compliment the objection with, "That's a great question, I'm glad you asked. . .and in addition to that, is there anything else that would prohibit your proceeding forward?" Again, the key after you ask a closing question is to be silent and allow him the opportunity to answer.

If the prospect responds, "No that's all," then you have arrived at the final objection. If, however, the prospect offers another objection, answer the objection, continue the process of asking, "In addition to that is there anything else," until the prospect acknowledges there are no more.

At this point compliment the prospect and his final objection. "Mr. Prospect, I understand and that makes perfect sense, so you tell me what would it take to satisfy your concerns."

Just Suppose...

The Just Suppose method of closing is also referred to as Handling the Final Objection Close. You have gotten the prospect to the point where he obviously wants and needs your product, but the final objection is causing him to hesitate.

With the Just Suppose Close, you remove the final objection as the reason for not going ahead.

If the prospect says, "I'm just not sure if your machine will perform as you say," you reply, "Mr. Prospect, I understand how you feel. Just suppose for a moment that I could satisfy all of your concerns in writing. Is there any other reason that would cause you not to become involved today?" At this point, he must either say no, or you uncover the real reason for not proceeding forward.

This is the perfect method for blowing past a smoke-screen objection and uncovering insincere objections. By incorporating "just suppose," the prospect will either agree or lead you to another objection. You will find you will either have him agreeing with you, or it will take you to the final objection.

Again, remain perfectly silent and listen to his entire concern. After his answer, you may consider employing the closing technique of "subject to" or "conditional terms" selling.

With "conditional terms" you have arrived at the final objection and the prospect says, "I need to check with my banker."

You reply, "Mr. Prospect, that makes perfect sense. Prior to your speaking with the banker, and to facilitate the transaction in a timely fashion, let's prepare the paperwork now, and we will make the sale subject to your banker's final approval. This way we can start the process, and if by chance, the bank does not agree with your decision, we will simply start over. That makes sense, doesn't it?"

You will never be closer to concluding the sale than at the very moment when you have arrived at the final objection. Instead of coming back at another time and taking a chance on the prospect's fears setting in and his emotions diminishing, ask for the order now instead of later.

The Mental Flip Flop is the prospect's psychological justification for purchasing your product or service. If the prospect makes the mental switch to that of a customer, then he psychologically enters into the process of justifying all the reasons why he will become an owner. Whereas, if you leave him thinking about the product as a non-owner, he does not think of reasons to go ahead, but dwells on his fears and thinks of all the reasons why he should not own.

Always attempt to conclude the transaction at the moment you answer the final objection. Even if it means making the sale subject to conditional terms. This way when you revisit to satisfy the conditions, you are coming back to a customer who has bought instead of a prospect who has been thinking about it.

Answer Objections in a Positive Manner

Discuss and answer all your objections tactfully and delicately. As mentioned earlier, an objection is just an unanswered question in a prospect's mind. Treat the question as a request for more information.

When you are offered an objection, remain calm, non-argumentative, and welcome the objection. Remember, it will be impossible to move into the closing sequence until you have answered all questions and concerns. Therefore, you want the prospect to feel free to object and to continue objecting until there are no more concerns.

Remember, when you first hear an objection, be enthusiastic and compliment the prospect, "Mr. Prospect, I'm glad you brought that up," or "Thanks for bringing that up," then answer the objection.

Feel, Felt, Found

Another way of handling an objection is with the feel, felt, found method. It's based on creating strong perceptions which reveal you to be understanding and empathetic. It also employs the closing techniques of third-party testimonial endorsements.

For instance, the prospect says, "I can get it elsewhere for less," or "I'm not in the market."

You respond, "Mr. Prospect, I understand how you feel, many others just like you felt the same way initially, but once they became an owner here is what they found...." Then you elaborate with a third-party testimonial of someone who was in the same situation or circumstances as they are, but as a result of going ahead with the decision to purchase they experienced great success and happiness.

If the objection is price, warranty, service or any other concern, the phrase, "I understand how you feel," sends a strong message to the prospect that you truly care.

Follow-up with a third-party endorsement of the happy customer, offering the proof the prospect needs to proceed forward. When the prospect says it's too expensive, you can respond, "Mr. Prospect, I understand how you feel, I recently had a customer who was in a similar situation and he felt the same as you. However, what he found as a result of owning was although the price seemed initially higher, our service and warranties far outweighed the value our competitor could offer.

"Tell me, is price your only concern or would reliable service and extended warranties also be important considerations?" Use this method and you can circumvent and turn around most any objection by empathy and the validity of a third-party testimonial.

Six-step Method to Overcoming Objections

Here are the six basic steps for handling objections or addressing questions and concerns. The system was popularized by the renown sales trainer J. Douglas Edwards. If followed it will almost always work in your favor during the objection process.

Step 1. Hear the objection out.

Do not interrupt, but listen entirely to the objection. Listen attentively with empathy and understanding. Give the prospect the opportunity to express his emotional concerns.

You have employed the Law of Six by identifying your six top objections and you have developed and internalized bullet-proof answers. However, you must not be too quick to answer. Though you may have heard the objection one thousand times before, it is this prospect's first time expressing his concerns for you.

Step 2. Repeat the objection back to the prospect.

This is a critical step! This strategy often helps the prospect answer his own objection as he hears it repeated back to him. State the objection out loud in a kind, non-threatening way.

When the prospect says, "it costs too much," repeat it back as a question: "It costs too much?" This method has several benefits.

✦ It makes your prospect feel important and understood.

✦ It verifies you heard the objection.

✦ By repeating the objection, you are in effect asking for more information.

Step 3. Question the objection.

Remember the first objections you hear may be masking a larger objection. Ask for elaboration. "Mr. Prospect, let me clarify my thinking or let me be sure I understand you correctly. If it were not for (objection), then would you proceed forward today? Is that right?" Remain silent and let him answer.

Step 4. Answer the objection with your pre-planned response.

Once you're confident you have the whole story behind his concern, you can state your pre-planned response with confidence.

Step 5. Confirm that the objection does not block the sale.

You have answered the objection, but you now must confirm the objection is no longer a reason for the prospect not to become a buyer.

✦ "That answers your question then, doesn't it Mr. Prospect?" or "That makes sense to you, doesn't it?"

If the prospect is not satisfied with your answer, now is the time to know. You cannot move forward and close until you are certain the issues are satisfied. If the prospect is satisfied, move to Step 6.

Step 6. Close.

It is important that you understand handling objections and closing are events that are occurring simultaneously. You overcome the objection and then move to the close.

✦ "Well then Mr. Prospect, do you have any additional questions before beginning the paperwork?"

✦ Prospect answers, "No."

✦ "Congratulations! I'm excited for you. By the way, will it be yours or your company name appearing on the agreements?"

The Final Word

The prepared salesperson should never loose a sale because of a customer's objections.

Vince Lombardi of the Green Bay Packers was one of the most triumphant coaches in football history. (I mentioned Vince in the introduction, discussing his focus on the basics.) His secret to success? Over preparation. Most professional events are won during the last two minutes of the game. While practicing, the Packers played five quarters, not the usual four. During the final quarter of the game when the opposing team began to wear down, the Packers exceeded the competition because they were mentally and physically prepared to go the extra mile.

You must be overly prepared to win at the objector's game.

Objections happen during the final minutes of the selling game, so it's not the time for you to wear down. Anticipate your objections, prepare your answers, internalize and memorize your reply; and you will move to the ranks of the super achiever.

7

Your Prospect Remains A Prospect Until You Close

Welcome to this section on concluding the sale. As a salesperson you can turn closing into an exciting and positive event.

You have discovered that selling consists of prospecting, qualifying, presenting, overcoming objections and the close—or the natural ending to successfully meeting the client's needs.

Make no mistake, closing is the bottom line. The result is you have a paycheck to deposit.

Before diving into the specific closing strategies and techniques here are some valuable tips.

Memorize the Closing Techniques

Once again, the professional salesperson is like the professional actor or actress with the closing methods well planted in his or her subconscious mind. Master your script before appearing on stage.

Have Your Closing Material With You . . . *Always*

Richard, an accomplished salesperson, excitedly proclaimed he had landed a sale that would net a $17,500 commission. I congratulated Richard, and asked for the contracts and deposit check so that we could process the paperwork. "Oh," he said, "I don't have them with me. As a matter of fact, I'm meeting the customer at the office in 30 minutes and we will prepare the contracts there."

I inquired, "Why didn't you prepare the agreements when you were with him?" I knew in advance what his response would be.

"I didn't have contracts with me, but don't worry they are solid. Besides, I would rather have the contracts typed."

I've experienced this scenario too many times but did not want to negate Richard's excitement. The point is: *be ready to close anytime, anywhere*! Contracts and business are to be concluded the moment the customer acknowledges acceptance.

In less than 10 minutes, Richard reappeared with the sullen look that required no explanation. The customer, now a prospect, had called with concerns. He would not be coming to the office and had decided to delay his decision. Richard would meet him later in the day to give him support information to pass on to his accountant and attorney.

Be ready to close anytime, anywhere, the moment your customer acknowledges acceptance. Keep your closing forms, calculator, pen and all other material with you at all times. Take them with you wherever and whenever you are with a prospect.

Remember, you have worked hard moving a prospect past his fear of making a mistake (buyer's remorse in advance). In an interim period, while you gather all your materials, doubt and fears have time to seep back in the prospect's mind and the sale could unravel quickly.

When you receive commitment, but decide to process the paperwork later, I promise you the client will have additional concerns you will have to address, and in some cases, you virtually will have to start your presentation over again. As difficult as it is the first time around, the second time the emotional odds will be against you.

Learn to Talk on Paper

I took this tip to heart from master salesperson and trainer Zig Ziglar. Zig suggests you always have a legal pad available during your presentation. He calls it "your talking pad."

Do you want to increase the power of your presentation twenty-two times, thus increase your probability of closing? Then learn to talk on paper. There are twenty-two times the nerve endings from the eye to the brain versus the ear to the brain and people naturally believe what's in the written over the spoken word.

In the vacation ownership industry, we had the saying, "Ink it, don't think it. Delegate to document," and when delivering a presentation we did a "pad talk." In other words, the presentation and its highlights were displayed in written form. The salesperson wrote any key benefits, warranties and assurances on his or her talking pad, and then let the prospect view it during a planned oral presentation. So combine an oral presentation with the power of the printed word.

When explaining math and figures to your prospect, always use a calculator, not a pen or pencil. Buyers assume your numbers are indisputable when you actually do the math right in front of them.

To increase your closing effectiveness, always carry a legal binder, which contains your contracts, calculator, pen and any other materials necessary to close.

Ask, and You Will Receive

Research conducted by Dr. Herb True of Notre Dame concludes that 46 percent of the people he interviewed ask for the order only once before giving up; 24 percent ask twice before shying away; 14 percent attempt to ask for the order the third time; and 12 percent continue to ask a fourth time before throwing in the towel. Thus 96 percent of the professional salespeople quit asking after somewhere between one and four closing attempts.

What's startling is the same research indicates that 60 percent of all sales occur after the fifth attempt of asking for the order. It's conclusive, the top four percent who possess the courage and technical skills to ask for the order after five attempts are making 60 percent of the sales as well as the commissions.

A Detroit newspaper reported a huge insurance policy had been purchased by Henry Ford. A friend of Mr. Ford's, who was also an insurance salesperson, naturally upset, inquired why he did not buy from him.

Take heed! Mr. Ford's answer holds the secret of sales success for anyone selling anything! He replied, **"You didn't ask me."**

For those of you who are hesitant to ask for fear of appearing like hard-sell, high-pressure salespeople you must bear in mind that asking for the order is the fundamental quality of the top sales professional. So, the critical closing instruction is to ask for the order. Ask enthusiastically. Ask confidently. And continue to ask until your invitation to own is accepted.

The Final Instruction . . .Silence

"The only pressure you are allowed to use in a sales presentation is the pressure of silence after you have asked the closing question."

—Brian Tracy

When you ask a closing question, it's critical you become perfectly silent and wait for the answer. Sounds easy, doesn't it? It was a difficult discipline for me to master and a challenge to convey to most new salespeople.

Why is it important to remain silent after asking a closing question? If you say anything prior to receiving a response, you take the pressure off the prospect to answer your closing question. If you remain silent after asking the closing question one of two things will occur:

1. Your prospect answers the closing question, committing to own.

2. Your prospect answers the closing question, giving you the reason he will not own.

Either answer is acceptable. If he commits, it's just a matter of completing the paperwork. If he does not commit, you are offered the reasons or concerns. This allows you the opportunity to overcome the objection and continue forward with the closing process until you conclude the sale.

What are the Closing Techniques and Strategies?

To understand what closing **is**, let's discuss what closing **is not**.

Closing techniques are not tactics of the cunning used to manipulate people into purchasing things they cannot use, don't want, can't afford or need.

Closing is a skill the professional salesperson possesses which leads people to decisions that benefit them. Understand the closing technique is designed to move a person or people involved in a decision past a moment of tension, indecision or fear.

Therefore, when you have given a presentation and the prospect is qualified, you are positively helping him or her make a decision to purchase a beneficial product or service, that otherwise, he or she may not make without your assistance.

8

The First Step of Closing: Get in the Door

Learning to secure the appointment is actually the first step to closing the sale. Here's where you can use the phone to your best advantage. It is still one of the best methods available to obtain appointments if you know how to use it properly.

Keep one golden rule regarding your telephone. **Never try to sell your product or service over the phone if a presentation or demonstration is necessary.** If a personal contact is required, or a presentation is necessary, then the only commitment you must gain over the phone is the appointment.

Usually there is a conflict every time you try to secure appointments by phone. The conflict is that your prospect wants to avoid an appointment with you, while you are trying to obtain an appointment with the prospect.

A phone to prospects is a tool to avoid an appointment. If prospects can persuade you to tell everything there is about your offering, plus the price, terms and availability of items, they will have accomplished their goal, which is to avoid a personal appointment with you.

A phone to salespeople is a tool to set and secure appointments. If you catch prospects' interest but don't tell them everything there is about your offering, such as price, terms and availability, then you will probably accomplish your goal—secure the appointment.

Interesting struggle isn't it? The prospect is trying to avoid the appointment and you are trying to secure it. But you know the prospect wants to avoid the appointment, so you are in a position to prepare your phone conversation in advance.

Prepare in advance by preparing for rejection. To set an appointment with the most successful people—those who are busiest and hardest to contact—you will have to overcome their objections. However, their objections (as we have discussed) are predictable. They are the same today as they have been for decades.

Here are some predictable objections your prospects will give to avoid an appointment and some responses to overcome them.

◆ **Time.** The number one objection or reason why no one wants to commit to an appointment is time. The people you need to see do not have large blocks of time. If you ever tell someone you need 30 minutes to one hour you will never get in the door.

You overcome the time objection in advance, before it is ever brought up, by selling small increments of time. **Sell minutes not hours.**

When asking for an appointment, be sure to convey you will only need a few minutes. "Mr. Prospect, it will only require 10 minutes." Successful people do not have hours to spare, and if they think their most guarded asset, time, will be monopolized, they will avoid you. So the key is to sell minutes, not hours, to overcome the time objection in advance.

✦ **To avoid the appointment the prospect will ask you to describe your offering over the phone.** Remember the golden rule: *Never try to sell your product if a presentation or demonstration is involved.*

"Mr. Prospect, I would like to explain to you over the phone what's involved, but I have something I must show you. I need just a few minutes of your time". . . then make the appointment.

✦ **To avoid the appointment your prospect will say: "I'll call you back."** Hopefully, you already realize "I'll call you back" is a brush off. If you don't realize that "I'll call you back" is, in most cases, a brush off, then I'll share my personal diet plan with you. The next time a prospect says he will call you back, resolve to miss a meal until he does call back. You will be a lot thinner by the time he gets back with you. It's never his responsibility to call you back. **All call backs and contacts are to be initiated by you.** When a prospect says, " I'll call you back," take control and say, "It would be much easier if I contacted you. I'm busy and in and out of the office, virtually impossible to reach. . . I'll call you back. When is a convenient time to speak again?"

◆ **To avoid the appointment your prospect will ask you to send your information in the mail.** Refuse to send your offering in the mail. That's another brush off, a nice way for the prospect to say I'm not interested, go away. If you are going to send it in the mail, save yourself the anxiety of rejection, stuff the envelope and send it to your own address. Do not delude yourself, thinking that mailing information and expecting a call back is proactive and you will make a sale. This is what you do say: "Mr. Prospect, I'd love to mail the information, but I have something I must show you. Why don't I drop it by personally?"

If he is at all interested, he will say it's all right to drop it by personally. You say "Will you be in this afternoon?" and go for scheduling the appointment with "I only need a few minutes of your time."

◆ **To avoid the appointment your prospect will suggest you call back.** You have worked hard to place yourself in touch with the primary decision maker. If he is trying to avoid the appointment, he may use his secretary or voice mail to screen your next call.

Prospect: *Call me back Monday, and we can get together some time next week.*

Salesperson: *Mr. Prospect, I have my calendar in front of me. Is your calendar handy? (The prospect is at his desk, of course he has* *it.) "Great, let's set an appointment right now. How about Wednesday, it will only take a few minutes, would 10 or 11 a.m. be convenient?*

Recently, I purchased a copier or rather I was sold a copier. Like many prospects, I was trying to shop by phone to obtain all the information and avoid the sales appointment.

First, I called my regular supplier. I had conducted business with him for years. My company had already purchased three copiers and two fax machines for the year, and my support staff normally handled these transactions. But this copier was for my home office, so I decided to handle the purchase myself. I called to get competitive bids, something I had not done in years. It was an easy process dealing with my regular supplier and I had everyone else fax me their information and give me their best price over the phone. However, there was one salesperson who refused to give me the information and insisted he had something he needed to show me and it would only require a few minutes of my time.

Needless to say he received the order, and I might add not on the issue of price, but on service. He proved his service in advance by just showing up.

Don't be put off with the predictable objections to avoid the appointment. Keep in mind if you cannot schedule something as simple as the appointment, you cannot complete something as major as the sale.

9

Closing Techniques: the Baker's Dozen

How many times do you ask before the person says yes? Statistics clearly indicate that closing usually occurs after the fifth attempt to ask for the order.

This is critical knowledge. If it takes a minimum of five closes to succeed, you will never lead a buyer to "yes" if you have only one or two closing techniques. When people ask me how many closing techniques they should memorize, I reply, "The super achiever normally has twenty plus closing strategies and techniques internalized."

You may say to yourself "why so many?" I suggest twenty plus techniques because every buying situation will be different, and each buyer's personality will be different.

To start out, here is the first group of closing techniques containing 13 of the most powerful tried and proven methods available to help your customer to agree. I suggest you learn the following closes in this chapter **word for word.**

When instructing future super achievers to learn the closes word for word, many of them resist. In case you may have the same objections, the following is a list of the most common ones.

Common Objections from Salespeople

1. *Some of the closing techniques will not work in my operation or some clash with my personality.*

   That's understandable, so use what's comfortable to yourself and to your operation. If you can only use a few of the following techniques, there will be more techniques offered further in the book. Build your closing armory with what's adaptable and comfortable.

2. *These are not my words, yet you expect me to learn them word for word.*

   I jokingly tell seminar audiences, "Of course they are not your words, it's my name, not yours appearing on the front cover of the book. So I ask you to learn the techniques word for word first, and then, through time and practice, you will adapt your own language style."

   (Several years ago a student approached me with a notebook of his favorite closing techniques. They were essentially the same techniques I had shared, yet after he memorized the original techniques, he rewrote and adapted the closing strategies to suit his selling situations and personality.)

3. *It is a lot of work to memorize word for word.*

I understand. I fought it too. But think of the alternative. If you continue to do business in the same manner, what kinds of results can you expect? If you continue to operate the same way, you can expect the same thing. You must expect to pay the full price in advance to experience the success you deserve, and the price is *hard work.*

Keep this thought in mind before deciding how many closing techniques you need to personally internalize and call your own.

If it takes over five attempts to make a sale, that means multiple techniques must be learned. Look at it this way: if you receive more objections than you have techniques, you will not get very far. Therefore, the reason you possess multiple techniques is to have more closes than they have objections. Use up their "nos" to lead them to "yes."

Let's get started, and by the way—have fun learning. Cultivate enthusiasm now. Carry it throughout the sales process. Remember, a sale is a transfer of enthusiasm.

I. THE ORDER FORM CLOSE

This is the fundamental closing technique. First, always have your contracts and order forms with you at all times. If you work from your desk, display them. If you keep your paperwork in sight, the prospects know you are not trying to hide anything. They also become accustomed to them if they come to your office more than once. It's easier for you too, if you have the necessary paperwork handy at the moment of closing. If you are delivering your presentation away from your desk, have a binder or attaché case with your legal pad and contracts readily available.

Why is the Order Form Close so effective? As you fill out the contract, you are not directly asking the prospect to buy (make a decision); you are simply making the decision for him.

The best time to work with this close is at the beginning and during your presentation. My favorite time to begin the Order Form Close is when the prospect asks a question that indicates a buying signal. You answer the question with a question of your own, and record the answer on the order form.

Prospect: *Does it come in red?*

Super achiever: *Mr. Prospect, would you like it in red?*

Prospect: *Yes, that's the color I want.*

Super achiever: *Let me make a note of that (record the information on your order blank or contract).*

As long as the prospect does not stop you from recording the answers on the contract, he is buying. But, if the prospect does stop and say something like:

Prospect: *Is that a contract? or, You are ahead of yourself, I'm not buying anything.*

Super achiever: *Of course you are not, I would never expect you to own without all the facts. I use this form to write all the information down. This form has everything about the offer arranged in a precise manner, such as price, terms, options, delivery date—all the information you and I both need for your review purposes later. That's okay, isn't it?*

From the start of the presentation to the end, "make a note" of all his questions and record terms on the order form. By the end of the presentation the contract is virtually completed and will only require a signature. Here's how this entire close is intended to work:

Prospect: *How much is the down payment?*

Super achiever: *Mr. Prospect, we would require an initial investment of either 10 or 20 percent, which would you prefer?*

Prospect: *I'd like to get in for the least amount, I suppose 10 percent.*

Super achiever: *Great, let me make a note of that.*

Prospect: *Is that a contract? You're getting ahead of yourself, I'm not ready to buy.*

Super achiever: *Of course you are not, I would never expect you to own without all the facts. This form has everything about the offering arranged in a precise manner, such as price, terms, options, delivery date—all the information you and I both need for your review purposes later. That's okay isn't it?*

Prospect: *Well, I guess that's okay.*

Super achiever: *By the way Mr. Prospect, we could schedule* *delivery for the first of the month if that fits into your time frame.*

Prospect: *Actually I would need it prior to the end of this month."*

Super achiever: *Mr. Prospect, I'm going to make note that delivery must occur by the 25th of this month, is that okay?*

Prospect: *Yes, that would work.*

Super achiever: *Mr. Prospect, would this purchase be under your company or personal name?*

Prospect: *I'd be purchasing this personally.*

Super achiever: *Outstanding! And your middle initial is?*

Prospect: *It's T.*

Super achiever: *What is the correct spelling of your mailing address?*

When you have asked all the questions and the contract is completely filled out, you review all the notes with the prospect and if he agrees, ask him to authorize or okay the agreement.

2. I WANT TO THINK ABOUT IT CLOSE

Sales trainer Tom Hopkins has his students memorize this technique word for word in his three-day boot camp sessions, and I personally feel if you do not commit this one close to memory you simply are not serious about the sales profession.

"I want to think about it" or "I want to think it over" are the most common objections a salesperson will encounter, regardless of the product offering. In the best of situations, under the most ideal conditions, you will hear these at least 50 percent of the time, so start committing this close to memory right away!

The prospect says "I want to think it over" for three reasons:

1. **It's a Brush Off:** Now swallow your ego and accept the fact that this prospect doesn't want what you're offering. Many times you are told "I want to think it over," because it's a nice way for him to send you on your way without hurting your feelings. The average salesperson is so vain he actually believes the prospect wakes up in the morning and goes to bed at night thinking over his offer. But, in reality when the salesperson calls back two or three days later, sure of a sale, the prospect doesn't even know who he is.

Now, let's suppose you are working with the genuinely interested prospect and he tells you "I want to think about it." This is what is occurring with the interested prospect who is hesitating.

2. **Buyer's Remorse in Advance:** At the moment of closing the prospect experiences tension. The tension is a fear of making a mistake, buying the wrong thing, paying too much or even being criticized by friends. These fears cause him to back away at the moment of closing and say "I want to think about it."

3. **Financial Resources:** He tells you he wants to think about it because of the price of the item or service. Don't be fooled, the

only reason, in most cases, he tells you "I want to think about it" is because he wonders if he can or should be able to afford your offer.

The problem with "I want to think about it" is it's a broad statement, not narrowed to any one specific concern. You are not down to the final objection and have nothing concrete to overcome. If you will follow this procedure, you will move beyond the vague generality of "think about it" to the final objection:

Prospect: *I need to think it over.*

Super achiever: *That's fine, obviously you would not take the time to think about it unless you were genuinely interested, would you? (Remain silent and wait for his reply. This question confirms he is genuinely interested.)*

Prospect: *Oh yeah, I'm definitely interested.*

Super achiever: *Great, since you are interested, I can assume you will give this careful consideration, won't you? (Remain silent and wait for the reply. His response, if he says yes, confirms he will actually think about it.)*

Prospect: *Yes, I definitely will be giving it the consideration it deserves.*

Super achiever: *Outstanding! Just to clarify my thinking, what phase of the offer is it you will be considering. Is it my company?*

Prospect: *No, your company's reputation is sterling.*

Super achiever: *Is it my service?*

Prospect: *No, you're service is outstanding, and you have performed beyond the call of duty.*

Super achiever: *Mr. Prospect, I sense you hesitating, do you mind my asking if it's the money?*

Rest assured if you have gotten him this far, and he is genuinely interested, in most instances, it will be a money issue. This being the case, bridge to the Money Close on page 134. Internalize and memorize it.

Here is the "I Want to Think About It Close":

Super achiever: *That's fine, obviously you wouldn't take the time to think about it unless you were genuinely interested, would you? Since you are genuinely interested, I can assume you will give this careful consideration. Just to clarify my thinking, what phase of the offer will you be considering? Is it my company? Is it my service? I sense your hesitancy, do you mind my asking, is it the money?*

Here is the key. Prospects do not think about your offer after you leave. They do not review your literature and product information. What they do is move on with their lives! The time to nail down the sale is at the end of your presentation when you have identified their needs and clearly presented your services as the solution to their needs.

Try the following techniques when you are working with people who have authoritative positions:

1. Prospect: *I want to think it over.*

Super achiever: *Mary, I'm sure a person in your position makes major decisions daily. You've made larger decisions than this before, haven't you? Isn't this relatively small in comparison to the decisions you have made in the past? Let's go forward with the decision now. I'll handle the details for you, and you're free to focus on the important issues of your business. That makes sense, doesn't it?*

2. Prospect: *I still need to think about it.*

Super achiever: *You impress me as a proactive decision maker. Why don't you and I take the bull by the horns to reach a decision right now?*

3. Prospect: *I still want to think about it.*

Super achiever: *Why invest more time thinking this over? You have told me that you are satisfied with the product and service. And that it's within the parameters of your budget. Haven't you thought about it already?*

4. Prospect: *I need to take more time to think this over.*

Super achiever: *I understand. Let's think out loud together. Share your reasons with me for not wanting to proceed forward.*

Remember the critical instruction. After you ask a closing question, remain perfectly silent and allow her time to answer.

3. INVITATIONAL CLOSE

This close is the first closing technique I learned primarily because of its simplicity. Yet, through the years it has become one of my all time favorite ways to ask for the order.

My two favorite questions with the Invitational Close are: "Why don't you give it a try?" or "Why don't you take it?" Either one is a delicate, yet powerful method that gently urges your prospect toward ownership.

You can use this close either at the end or during your sales presentation to conclude the transaction. It will be preceded by a trial close such as, "Mr. Prospect, how do you like it?" or "Mr. Prospect, do you have any further questions?"

Super achiever: *Mrs. Prospect, how do you like the copier?*

Prospect: *I do like it.*

Super achiever: *Great, why don't you give it a try?*

Inviting the prospect to make a buying decision is a low-key method that bridges to the decision to own. With my consulting and seminar services I might say, "John, increased productivity makes sense to you, doesn't it? Why don't you give our services a try?"

The more direct invitational close is "Why don't you take it?" I suggest this close to real estate sales professionals when showing properties. After demonstrating and presenting a home in its entirety ask:

Super achiever: *Bill, Mary, how do you like the home?*

Prospects: *We absolutely love it.*

Super achiever: *Great, why don't you take it?*

One of two things will occur. The prospects will answer yes and you will congratulate them, and move rapidly to the Order Form Close to complete the contracts. In the event they say no or hesitate, you simply ask, "Why not?" The prospects then will explain to you what it is they are looking for. Now, you have just identified their hot button.

4. HOT BUTTON CLOSE

The Hot Button Close is founded on the 80/20 rule which states that 80 percent of all results come to bear on 20 percent of energy expended. In sales we say 80 percent of the sales are made by the top 20 percent of the sales team, whereas the other 20 percent of the sales volume is shared by the remaining 80 percent of the sales force. Because this is the irrefutable case in all sales organizations, I always advise people in management to invest 80 percent of their time with the top 20 percent of the sales team to maximize results.

The 80/20 rule in selling products or services is based on the fact that 80 percent of the buying decision will be based on 20 percent of the product's features. In other words, if you have ten product features, your job is to find the one or two features that represent the key benefits to the person buying your product, and push his hot button over and over again.

Every time you speak of your product in terms of the prospect's hot button, you are speaking his language and igniting his enthusiasm. Conversely, when you talk to the customer about things that are of no interest to him, buying desire rapidly diminishes.

The Beautiful Flowering Cherry Tree
An Example of Hot-button Selling

A real estate professional shows an older home to a couple. The home is in need of some repair. Upon arriving they see a beautiful flowering cherry tree in the front yard. The wife, who seems to be the more dominant one, says to her husband, "Look Tom, a beautiful flowering cherry tree. When I was a young girl, my family home had a beautiful cherry tree, and I've always dreamed our home would have a tree just like this one."

Tom nudges his wife and says, "Let me handle this, I'll do the talking."

The salesperson identifies the hot button, makes a mental note and prepares the presentation.

Tom is playing reluctant buyer and says, "The deck needs immediate repair." The salesperson agrees, "Yes, but from your deck, you would always enjoy the view of the beautiful flowering cherry tree." They go through the house and Tom says, "The carpet needs to be replaced and the house needs to be painted." The salesperson replies, "You're right, but from the bay window you have a glorious view of the beautiful flowering cherry tree." Upon viewing the master bedroom, Tom objects, "The bedroom is small and the bathroom needs new fixtures."

"Yes, but from here you have a perfect view of the beautiful flowering cherry tree." At the end of the showing, Mrs. Prospect, who loves the beautiful flowering cherry tree, convinces her husband to buy the home.

The cherry tree was the hot button and the emotional key which was pushed over and over until the decision was rendered. If you question skillfully and listen intently, the buyers will tell you exactly what will make them purchase your offer. Not only will they tell you what will cause them to own, but what would cause them not to own.

Pay strict attention to the buying signal, determine the key benefits, and build your sales presentation around the hot button.

❖ ❖ ❖

5. ASSUMPTIVE CLOSE

All top sales professionals are assumptive closers. From the beginning of the presentation to the end, they confidently assume the buyer will own even before they have received confirmation or acknowledgment that a buying decision has been reached.

The Assumptive Close is sometimes referred to as "the next step close." Have you ever been in the middle of your presentation and the prospect says, "What's the next step?" It may not happen often but when it does, it's time to be assumptive, swing into the Order Form Close and begin wrapping up the details.

> **Prospect:** *What's the next step?*

> **Super achiever:** *Mr. & Mrs. Prospect, I'm glad you asked. The next step is for you to authorize the agreements, and I will need a check for $1,000 as the deposit on your investment.*

If the prospect does not ask what the next step is, then initiate the Assumptive Close at the end of your sales presentation by first issuing a Trial Close:

> **Super achiever:** *Mr. & Mrs. Prospect, do you have any additional questions before we begin the paperwork?*

> **Prospects:** *No.*

> **Super achiever:** *Great, then I need you to authorize the agreements and write a check for $1,000 as a deposit on your investment.*

Pay strict attention! You have just been given the most powerful Assumptive Close in your sales career. That is the strategy of the "No Close." This close was developed by sales trainer Bob Schultz and actually elicits the response a salesperson fears most, which is "No." With this technique, you gently nudge the prospect into saying no:

> **Super achiever:** *Do you have any questions before we begin the paperwork.*

> **Prospect:** *No.*

> **Super achiever:** *Great. Then the next step is for you to authorize*

the agreements and make out a check for $1,000 as a deposit on your investment.

From here you simply begin processing the contracts. You would be surprised at the vast numbers of prospects who agree to "yes" by saying "no." If, for any reason the prospect does object, you overcome the objection and then ask for the order again.

To be an assumptive closer, the sale must first occur in your mind before it occurs in the prospect's mind. Its power is in the psychological principle that your assumptive attitude creates the prospect's desire for your product. The stronger your positive assumptive attitude that the sale is inevitable, the greater the probability the prospect will own.

Assumptive Closes to Memorize

1. *Mr. Prospect, prior to our meeting I took the liberty to prepare the paperwork. All that is needed is for you to authorize the agreements.*

2. *We seem to be in agreement on all the major points. When would you like to schedule delivery?*

3. *This has been an incredible meeting, and I look forward to working with your company during the upcoming year. The initial investment is $5,000. Would you be taking care of the deposit with a personal or company check?*

B

The Assumptive Handshake Close
(A Variation on the Assumptive Close)

The handshake represents a person's word, integrity and psychologically bonds an agreement. This has been the case since the beginning of time.

Larry, a super salesperson, assumptively concluded an expensive vacation home transaction with the handshake. At the end of the presentation, after covering countless objections, the husband looked to his wife and said, "What do you think?" The chances were high the wife could have responded with, "I think we should think it over." Before a reply was given, Larry assumptively looked at them both and offered his assurances, "I think you have made a wise decision. Congratulations." He then shook hands with both the husband and wife and they accepted.

It's important to note the buyers were both qualified, their needs determined, and the solution was presented. Yet, as in most cases, there was hesitancy. The moment of tension was relieved and the sale concluded by the Assumptive Handshake Close.

6. ALTERNATIVES CLOSE

This close automatically concludes the sale by offering the prospect two or more alternatives. You offer a choice between something and something rather than a choice between something and nothing.

Earlier, we discussed in depth the buyer's fears and that "no" is usually a natural ingrained response—nothing more than a knee-jerk reaction. You never ask the prospect, "Do you want this or not?" This allows the prospect to say no. Instead, you say "Would you prefer, item A or B?" Either answer (item A or item B) is a "yes" decision.

One of the great sales trainers of all time, Elmer Wheller, employed the Alternatives Close to save Walgreens Drug Store from near disaster during the height of the depression.

The Walgreen Story

Walgreen had gone from successful to barely surviving as most businesses did during the depression. They called the brilliant salesperson and trainer Mr. Wheller and asked, "Can you help our salespeople sell in this depression?"

Mr. Wheller asked Walgreens the critical question, "What's your most profitable and easiest item to sell?"

The store manager responded, "Eggs." Mr. Wheller observed their sales process and heard the clerks asking, "Do you want an egg in your drink or not?" Of course the natural response was "No."

To remedy this, he had them change the question to a choice. "Do you want one egg or two in your drink?"

Suddenly Walgreens went from no eggs to at least one egg in every drink. This Alternative Close resulted in an incredible profit increase for Walgreens.

Depending upon the circumstances, there are several ways to present an Alternatives Close:

◆ Delivery:

This could be delivered and installed in your office this upcoming

Friday, or would Monday morning be more convenient?

Closing on your new home could occur in 30 days or would you prefer to delay for 60 days?

✦ **Finances:**

The initial investment would be secured by cash or personal check, which would you prefer?

Ms. Prospect, we could defer billing for 30 days, or if you were to pay cash now we could offer a five percent discount. What works best for you?

Would you like me to send this C.O.D? Do you prefer to charge to MasterCard or Visa?

✦ **Options and Features:**

We have two options to choose from, the walnut or the oak finish. Which would best compliment your office?

Would you prefer pre-owned or brand new?

✦ **Appointments:**

I have either Monday or Wednesday available for this week. What works best for you. . .My office or yours? How about 10 a.m. or 12 noon for lunch?

Learn to offer two choices to your prospect. Ask, "Do you want this or do you want that?" When the question is answered it's the perfect opportunity to "make a note" which leads you to your Order Form Close.

7. TRIAL CLOSE

The purpose of the Trial Close is to evaluate and determine where you are with your prospect during the presentation.

Unlike a close that concludes the transaction, in a Trial Close you are not at the point of asking for the order and the money, but merely seeking the prospect's opinion, and the willingness to buy, prior to moving into the final close. Actually, asking for opinions (Trial Close) is something you perform throughout the presentation to check the prospect's readiness to own. Here are examples:

How are we doing so far?

Is this what you had in mind?

Is this what you are looking for?

Does this make sense to you?

Is this an improvement over what you are doing?

The benefit of the Trial Close is the prospect can answer yes or no. Because you are merely "testing the waters," you don't end the presentation. Great salespeople use this close throughout the presentation to "take the prospect's buying temperature."

"Mr. and Mrs. Prospect, is this what you are looking for?" If they say no, you say, "Fine, what is it you are looking for?" It's like traveling down a forked road. "Does this make sense to you?" They confirm and you move to the next fork in the road. "You like the colors?"

Then you move to the next fork, "Is this what you like?" Follow the road to the final close.

The basic process of selling is asking questions, determining hot buttons, gaining commitments, and Trial Closes solidify the questions you ask.

Trial Closes to Memorize

1. Super achiever: *I get the impression you are excited about the opportunity presented? Is that correct?*

2. Super achiever: *Mr. & Mrs. Prospect on a scale of 1 to 10, 1 meaning owning may not make complete sense yet, and 10 being it makes perfect sense. . .where are you on the scale of 1 to 10?*

Prospect: *I guess we're at a 7.*

Super achiever: *Great. What additional information will you need to help you get to a 10?*

3. Super achiever: *Now that I have demonstrated the features of the machines, how do you feel they will benefit your operation?*

4. Super achiever: *Mr. Prospect, why is it you want to own?*

5. Super achiever: *After viewing the features and benefits, wouldn't you agree it's unnecessary to even consider owning anything else?*

8. BEN FRANKLIN CLOSE

OK, I know what you are thinking, the Ben Franklin Close is as old as the hills, everybody is familiar with it. This does not negate the fact it's still the most powerful close that has ever been developed for the sales profession. And for good reason.

The Ben Franklin Close parallels how humans process information and think. Whenever we are faced with a decision, we run through a check-and-balance system to weigh the pros and cons of the decision. We look for a reason to do something or not to do it.

Ben Franklin, who was America's first self-made millionaire, made his decisions by first taking a piece of paper and drawing a line down the center. On one side he wrote all the reasons favoring the decision, and on the other side he wrote his reasons for opposing it. Then, he would review his list and render a careful decision.

The reason why salespeople fight this technique is because they think it's an outdated method. However, here is how you can use the *improved* Ben Franklin Close.

> **Super achiever:** *Mr. & Mrs. Prospect, I can sense you are having difficulty with this decision, aren't you? (Silence, wait for reply). The last thing I would want is for you to make a choice you might be uncomfortable with. May I make a suggestion? Let's use a systematic decision-making method. On one side of my legal pad we will list the reasons favoring a positive decision, and on the other side we'll list your concerns. Afterward, we'll see if it makes sense to you.*

As the super achiever, take your pen and paper and fill out all the reasons for owning for your prospect. Then make a Summary

Close (page 153); restating all the positive reasons for owning. The pen is in your hand and you are the one writing. You should be able to come up with countless reasons why they should own. After you fill out the positive reasons, you say, "It certainly seems as if there are a number of good reasons for going forward, doesn't it?" (Wait for the reply.)

Now you simply hand them the pen and paper and say, "Now that we've listed all the reasons for, can you think of any reasons not to go ahead?" (The key now is to remain perfectly silent and let them work on it by themselves.) Most of the time, they will not be able to list more than three to four reasons to prohibit owning.

From here you begin to Assumptively Close by saying something like: "Looks like you have made the right decision," or "It seems pretty obvious doesn't it?" Progress to the Order Form Close.

The Ben Franklin Close should not be limited to the end of your presentation when trying to gain the final commitment. In my former real estate development career, the home-building division was highly competitive, so when prospects suggested they were considering the services of another builder, I asked two questions that triggered a Ben Franklin Close:

Super achiever: *Mr. & Mrs. Prospect, builder XYZ does a fine job. I'm curious, can you tell me what services and features they offer that cause you to want to do business with them?*

Is there any reason or concerns that would cause you not to have that company construct your dream home?

The first purpose of the questions is to understand their hot buttons (everything they are looking for in a builder). Second, they give what is called the " inverse hot button"— the reasons why they would not want to use a particular builder. From this you would develop your presentation to satisfy their hot buttons, as well as their concerns.

This is a magnificent close, whether selling simple or complex products and services. When a person has difficulty making a decision, normally he has moved past his emotional high and is attempting to justify the purchase by logic. The *improved* Ben Franklin Close will satisfy even the most discriminating, analytical person.

9. THE PUPPY DOG CLOSE

What do puppy dogs have to do with closing? Let's examine how smart pet store owners used to sell cute little puppy dogs. You let the prospect "give the puppy dog a try" and take it home on a trial basis.

Pet Store Sales Story

A parent and her children unexpectedly walk into the pet store just to look at the puppy dog they saw in the window. The children begin chanting: "We want the puppy dog, we want the puppy dog!"

The pet store owner takes the dog from the display window and the parent and children become emotionally involved with a purchase decision that they probably had not even considered before walking into the store. The children persist with, "Please Mommy, can't we have the puppy dog? We'll take care of it. Can't we take it home with us?"

The store owner senses her apprehension and then issues the Invitational Close:

"This is a major decision, so why don't you just give it a try? Take the puppy home for a few days and play with him! If you don't feel comfortable, just bring him back." The parent reluctantly agrees, thinking it's no obligation, we'll just "give it a try" and bring it back in a couple of days after the kids discover they really don't want the responsibility of a dog.

But what usually happens is the puppy dog takes on an identity and is given a name. It looks up at everyone with those soft brown eyes, and cuddles in each family member's lap. The kids are enamored. The parents are smitten. Suddenly, that cute little puppy dog is a part of the family and the sale is consumated.

Powerful close! Wouldn't you agree? And some of the most successful companies in the world use this type of sales close.

Remember, I told you the story of the salesperson who helped me purchase my copy machine. Being no dummy, he noticed I was operating in my home office with an outdated thermal-paper fax machine. He asked for the fax-machine order too, and my knee-jerk ingrained response was, "No, I've spent all I am going to spend on the copy machine. The fax machine will come later." However, on the day he delivered my copier, he also closed the fax-machine sale by employing the Puppy Dog Close.

"Now, Mr. Barnes, I know you mentioned you weren't quite ready for a new fax machine, but this was at the warehouse, and I just wanted to see how you feel about using the features of a laser, plain-paper fax machine. Just give it a try, I'll be back in about 30 days to inspect the copier and if the fax machine is not for you, it won't cost you a cent. You can determine if you would like to own a machine like this or continue with your old one."

Guess who now owns a laser, plain-paper fax machine? And what's the lesson? As a sales educator and consultant, I saw the close coming from a mile away. Yet, when your tactics are sound, and you have the best interests of your customer in mind, even if they know what you are doing, you are invincible.

Let's drive the point home again. A sale is emotional and to peak emotional responses, you must let the prospect see, touch, feel, smell, hear the benefits of your product or service. That's why it's imperative, whenever possible, to place your product in the hands of the prospect so he can experience, first hand, the emotional values.

In the vacation ownership industry, they invite you for a "free complimentary, no obligation weekend" to decide if owning a share in a condominium fits your philosophy and lifestyle. You arrive, the salespeople greet you with a bottle of wine and show you a luxury, two-bedroom villa, complete with jacuzzi and huge, wall-to-wall mirrors in the master bedroom. Prior to meeting your representative, you enjoy the health club while the children are at the pool. The representative meets with you and really doesn't attempt to close, but says, "Now isn't this what you deserve? Wouldn't it be nice to treat your family like this forever? By the way, I have a very special home just like this one. Why don't you give it a try?"

If you sell automobiles, let them test drive the car. If you represent real estate, get them in the home and on the property. If you market boats, put them in the water. The Puppy Dog Close is so overwhelmingly appealing, the salesperson does little work to conclude the sale. The buyers close themselves, because experiencing the product makes them feel like an owner even before they commit to saying yes.

10. THE SHARP ANGLE CLOSE

The Sharp Angle Close, sometimes referred to as the "If I could, would you?" close, is a superb maneuver when confronted with most types of objections. Whatever the concern you receive, you simply "sharp angle" the objection and send it back to the prospect with "If I could, would you?"

> **Prospect:** *I don't know if I can afford it.*

> **Super achiever:** *Mr. Prospect, if I could offer low, convenient monthly terms, would you proceed?*

The Sharp Angle close is also a perfect method to handle smoke-screen objections. I discussed in the objections portion of the book that sometimes the prospect's first objection may not be the real or final objection. Observe how to smoke out the hidden objection with "If I could, would you?"

Prospect: *I don't know if I can afford it.*

Super achiever: *Mr. Prospect, if I could offer low, convenient monthly terms, would you proceed?*

Prospect: *Is that possible?*

(The average salesperson would be tempted to jump in and answer yes. The super achiever takes the opportunity to make sure she's handled the final objection and is not so quick to answer.)

Super achiever: *I can't be certain until we process a loan application. I have an application which will only take a moment to complete, and we can make the sale "subject to" financial approval. That makes sense, doesn't it?*

Prospect: *I don't know, I probably need to think about it.*

Super achiever: *Mr. Prospect, I sense your hesitancy. In addition to the financial arrangements is there something else that prohibits you from becoming involved today?*

Prospect: *Well, I just want to be certain it will perform to your claims and as specified.*

(The super achiever now issues a second Sharp Angle Close.)

Super achiever: *Mr. Prospect, I understand how you feel. In addition to the terms, if I could offer full written warranty assurances, would you proceed today?*

Prospect: *Well, under those terms, it seems reasonable.*

(Note: The super achiever now begins to conclude the sale by assumptively employing three additional closing techniques, the Assumptive Handshake Close, the Order Form Close, and the Alternatives Close.)

Super achiever: *Congratulations Mr. Prospect you've made a wise decision. (Assumptive Handshake Close)*

Prospect: *Thank you.*

Super achiever: *The next step is to simply prepare the paperwork. May I have the correct spelling of your full name? (Order Form Close)*

Prospect: *John A. Smith*

Super achiever: *Mr. Smith, about the initial investment, will you be handling the deposit with credit card or personal check? (Alternatives Close)*

Prospect: *Credit card.*

Closes Are Stacked on Top of One Another

It is vitally important you review the previous closing scenario numerous times. There is an important underlying lesson contained within. Realize, that although we began with the Sharp Angle Close, this was not the technique that concluded the sale. The Sharp Angle was only a preceding close that lead to the final closing strategies of the Assumptive Handshake Close, Order Form Close and Alternatives Close.

Take heed and pay close attention to the next statement. The importance of knowing multiple closing techniques is because no one close concludes the sale—it requires the use of many closing techniques.

You will notice we stacked and layered technique upon technique, each close building on the preceding close until the sale was complete. You must note we never directly asked the prospect to buy, we lead him to the decision with closing questions. Let's review:

◆ *I can't afford it.*
   Sharp Angle—If I could, would you proceed today?

◆ *How can I be certain of performances and your claims?*
   Sharp Angle—If I could would you go forward today?

◆ *I need to think about it.*
   Think About It Close—In addition to that is there anything else?

◆ **Assumptive Handshake Close:** Congratulations and assurances.

◆ **Order Form Close:** Assumptively closing

◆ **Alternatives Close:** Asking for the money—cash, check or credit card.

As you can see, many techniques were employed: (1 & 2 Sharp Angle Close twice, 3) Think About It Close, 4) Assumptive Handshake Close, 5) Order Form Close and 6) Alternatives Close. Remember the statistics that said the average sale is concluded after the fifth attempt? Asking for the order and getting it requires techniques and having a preplanned, scripted methodology to guide the buyer into a beneficial decision that normally his own fears would have prohibited.

11. THE MINOR POINT CLOSE

This close, oftentimes referred to as the Secondary Close, is based on the premise that it's easier to have the customer make a small decision rather than ask for the major commitment to buy your product or service. You ask for commitment on a minor detail, the acceptance of which indirectly propels the prospect to agree on the major decision.

Minor Point Closing Examples

✦ **Automobile:** Would you like cloth or vinyl seats?

✦ **New Home:** Would you like to ask that the window treatments be included with your offer to purchase?

✦ **Finance:** Would that be cash or charge?

In the above cases, interior finishes or methods of payment are minor issues, but if the prospects agree to the minor decisions, the major decision to commit to the entire offering naturally follows.

12. THE YES MOMENTUM CLOSE

This great close consists of asking your prospects questions that lead them to answer yes. Super achievers know that if their prospects get into a mental pattern of saying yes from the very beginning of their presentation, it will become very difficult for them to say no at the closing.

The goal of the Yes Momentum Close is to create an atmosphere of agreement. To do this, you first need to tie down the close by asking questions at the beginning or end of a sentence that demands a yes answer. It psychologically ties your prospect into a yes agreement.

Whenever you state anything about your company, product or service, the prospect has a tendency to not believe you. It's your job to present your offer in the best light. Tom Hopkins says, "If you say it, they doubt it, if they say it, it's true." Therefore, the benefit of a tie down is the prospect verbally agrees with your statements, and then comes to believe what she is saying.

Tie Down Words

Doesn't it	Hasn't she
Isn't that right	Won't they
Wasn't it	Aren't they
Couldn't it	Shouldn't it
Wouldn't it	Can't you
Aren't you	Don't you agree
Won't you	Isn't it
Haven't they	Didn't it

Types of Tie Downs

◆ Deductive Tie Downs are the most common and are used at the end of a sentence to demand yes.

Super achiever: *It's a tremendous value, wouldn't you agree?*

Prospect: *Yes.*

✦ **Inverted Tie Downs** occur at the beginning of a sentence. It is less demanding and leads a prospect to say yes.

> **Super achiever:** *Isn't it exactly what you have in mind?*

> **Prospect:** *Yes.*

✦ **Internal Tie Downs** are used in the middle of your statements of fact.

> **Super achiever:** *Mr. & Mrs. Prospect, as we stand here on the bridge, can't you imagine how you and your family will enjoy this new boat for years to come?*

> **Prospects:** *Yes.*

✦ **Tag on Tie Downs:** Whenever your prospect offers positive statements, add a tie down in your response that bolsters value.

> **Prospect:** *The views are absolutely incredible!*

> **Super achiever:** *Aren't they?*

Start your presentation and conversation positively, and lead your prospects in agreement beginning with your greeting. "Welcome, thank you for the opportunity to meet. It's a great day, isn't it?" Building numerous small agreements from the beginning of your presentation to the end will lead you to the final positive close, "This is what you want, isn't it?"

Examples of Tie Downs

> *I bet you are surprised with what this machine will accomplish, aren't you?*

Isn't this what you have always dreamed of owning?

It's a sound investment strategy, wouldn't you agree?

Don't you agree, this is exactly what your specifications call for?

You are excited now, aren't you?

Based on what we have shared, it fits your needs perfectly, doesn't it?

13. REFERRAL PROSPECTING CLOSE

There are only two ways you can increase your business. One, find new prospects daily and two, obtain more business from your existing customer base.

The easiest and most effective method of obtaining new prospects is to gather referrals. Why is a referral so much more powerful than a cold call? Because it makes you more credible. Earlier, we discussed there are actually three factors the prospect considers during the sales process. First is you as the salesperson, second, your company and third, your product or service. If you obtain a referral from a satisfied customer, your credibility is already established.

In addition to your credibility being established, like-minded people usually associate with one another. This is referred to as the "nest factor" and the nest factor simply says "birds of a feather flock together." This means if your customer is qualified to own, then he is most likely associating with and referring qualified buyers to you.

The optimum time to obtain referrals is either immediately after the purchase or at the time of delivery. The key to obtaining referrals is this: No one volunteers referrals. You must ask for them.

A

Super achiever: *Mr. & Mrs. Customer, I have a favor to ask you.*

Customers: *Sure, what is it?*

Super achiever: *With my business, my most valued resource is the customer. My top priority is knowing you are satisfied. You are satisfied and comfortable with your investment decision, aren't you?*

Customers: *We certainly are.*

Super achiever: *Then, the favor I ask is this. I would like to share the same opportunity with your friends or relatives. Do two to three persons come to your mind who would enjoy the same benefits as you?*

(Note: You have asked for referrals that come to mind immediately with the Alternatives method. Normally they will choose two because it's easier than three.)

After you obtain the names you ask for the phone numbers and if the customer is extremely comfortable with you, ask that he call ahead to introduce you, your company and services.

Another method for referral prospecting comes from a friend of mine in the insurance business. This is how he asks for referrals:

B

Super achiever: *Mr. Customer, if your best friends were present right now, would you introduce us to one another?*

Customer: *Certainly, I'd be glad to.*

Super achiever: *Mr. Customer, that's exactly what I'd like to ask you to do. Would you mind if I called to introduce myself and my service to two or three of your best friends?*

There is one final method to the Referral Prospecting Close and that is to obtain prospects from people who did not buy. Julie, an outstanding salesperson, always asks for referrals from non-buyers in the following fashion:

C

Super achiever: *Mr. Prospect, I understand the timing is not right to own now, (or I understand you are not in a position to become involved, or I understand you are not in a position to decide today) but could you give me the names of two or three people you think may be able to take advantage of my services?*

Remember, you earn referrals by excellent service. If you have followed through and satisfied the customer with good service and positive results, you have earned the right to ask for referrals.

10

You Are Not A Salesperson If You Give It Away

It is a misconception that customers are only concerned with the lowest price. Many salespeople and business owners think this is so. If this misconception were true, companies selling high-priced, luxury-type items would not make a profit. What use would a salesperson be if the customer purchased only the cheapest item? We wouldn't need salespeople—just more sophisticated telephone answering machines so customers could simply place their orders.

So, as a salesperson, you must realize customers are concerned with more than price even though you often hear them ask, "How much is it?" when you haven't fully described your offering yet.

"How much is it?" (appearing early in the presentation) is just as frustrating as the prospect's response, "It costs too much," "It's more than I expected," "I can't afford it," "Your competition is cheaper," or the classic, "I'll be back."

As with many objections, price, as a concern, is predictable. Your prospects and customers will always want to know "How much is it?" early on. And once they know, they often complain. When you realize that price resistance is a natural, predictable objection, you are on your way to the top of your profession.

The Basics of Price Resistance

1. **It always costs too much.** A price objection is an automatic response. Everybody asks how much it is and then flinches at the price. All consumers, yourself included, become intoxicated with the idea of obtaining the best value possible. So, no matter what the cost, the initial reaction is "it's more than we expected to pay."

2. **Price is the common denominator.** Why does price come up early in the sales presentation? It's because it represents something we all have in common and that is a concern with money. We all relate to dollars and cents.

As a salesperson you must be clear: **Is price their objection or yours?** Often the price objection appears in the salesperson's mind first. Rest assured, if you are uncomfortable with the price, then you won't be able to overcome the objection in the prospects' mind.

Someone else is always selling something similar to your product for less. Any low level order-taker, other than a professional salesperson, can "give away" the product or service at a lower price. The sign of a super salesperson is someone who can represent the product at the higher value.

Unless You Are Selling Commodities, Price Is Never the Only Concern

What is a commodity? Let's use soybeans as an example. Suppose one farm produced 60,000 tons of beans, and then sold the beans to three separate brokers for the same price. The three brokers then market the same bean from the same farm to a grocery store chain. Would the grocery store consider price as the only factor?

Say two of the three distributors offered the same price under the same terms but at a lower price than the third distributor. The third distributor, however, offers the following services:

1. **Service call on a monthly basis.** The other distributors, #1 and #2, don't make calls.

2. **Delivery.** Distributors #1 and #2 require the customer to pickup.

3. **Warranty.** No warranty with #1 and #2. The sale is final.

4. **Terms.** Distributors #1 and #2 offer a cash-only sale.

Remember, the beans came from the same farm, have the same grain, texture and flavor. Yet, through differentiation (value-added service) the third distributor is able to outsell the competition regardless of price. Your job is to differentiate yourself, and your product and price will never again be the only concern to conclude the sale.

What Do Customers Buy?

The Sales Representative: The customer never has the opportunity to experience the product or company until he or she first "buys" the salesperson. To the customer, you represent the product and company, and you have tremendous influence over the customer's decision to own.

Service (Added Value): There are two types of sales organizations, those who are price driven and those who are service and value driven. The price-driven company and salesperson operate on the "one-night-stand philosophy"—get in, get out. This type of company does not care about developing customer relationships. They sell only to customers who buy low price, not service and responsibility. Whereas, the service-value-driven company most likely has long-term customers and referrals.

Delivery: If you can deliver on time with predictability, you can often overcome the price objection. Dominos pizza, for instance, dominated the market with the most expensive pizza, but their one giant selling differential was on-time delivery.

Warranties: Many products today require the services of technicians. A major fear for many consumers is being stuck with a machine—fax, computer, phone system—which fails. Providing outstanding service and warranties to assure customer satisfaction overcomes price sensitivity.

Remember, the customer will always initially think your price is too high. Therefore, differentiation of your product or service and the willingness to show value in comparison to what else is available is essential.

When Is Price Discussed?

For the most part, even if your prices are boldly displayed in your sales brochures, do not discuss cost until the end of your presentation. I am not suggesting evasiveness, but keep in mind that it will always "cost too much" until you build value, which can only be accomplished by discussing the benefits throughout your presentation.

Here's an example of how to overcome the "How much is it?" question before you have a chance to fully explain what the prospect will get for his money:

Prospect: *How much is it?*

Super achiever: *Mr. Prospect, is price your only concern?*

Prospect: *Well, no.*

Super achiever: *If it's all right with you, can we discuss that after I've had the opportunity to determine what your exact needs are? Is that OK?*

In the case where you do receive an objection, and the prospect says price is the primary concern, try the following scenario:

Prospect: *How much is it?*

Super achiever: *Mr. Prospect, is price your only concern?*

Prospect: *As a matter of fact, it is. I'm looking for the best deal.*

Super achiever: *Really, I'm surprised! Most customers have a lot of other concerns such as service, warranties and delivery schedules. Would service and warranties be issues you would be considering as part of the purchase decision or is price still your only concern?*

Prospect: *Well, no I'm interested in service and your warranty also.*

Super achiever: *Great. Allow me to address your warranty and service concerns first, and we will discuss the best value in just a moment. Is that OK?*

With my former construction and housing development career, we were hands down the highest-priced builder for a variety of reasons. When you build homes that cost half a million to one million dollars, the materials used are of substantially better quality than those used in lesser-priced homes.

Our predictable price question early on in the presentation was "What does it cost per square foot to build?" or "What's your price per square foot?" The way to handle price resistance is to kick the chair out from underneath the objection by answering the question in advance of being asked.

Super achiever: *Mr. & Mrs. Prospect, before we begin, I'd like to mention that most of our customers' first question is, "How much per square foot will it cost to construct our new home." Is that a question you have today?*

Prospect: *Yes, we are wondering about the cost per square foot.*

Super achiever: *Great, but unfortunately the cost of your new home will not be determined by the square foot. What will determine the value of your home are the component parts such as the materials used to construct your home. There are major price differences in items such as floor coverings, fixtures, and exterior and interior finishes. What we need to first determine is what you would like in your home. The price will be determined by the materials we use. That makes sense, doesn't it?*

Sometimes if you are representing higher prices relative to your competition and you know it will surface early as an objection, it's best to address it in advance!

You Never Pay Too Much For Something You Really Want

Simply put, intense desire to own reduces the price substantially. Yet, we all know, even if some prospects ardently desire what you're offering, you will still hear objections such as, "It costs too much." For some people wearing down a salesperson is a sport and to negotiate is a way of life. And, of course, a method to offer reassurance to themselves is that they are receiving the best value available.

One of the greatest responses to "It costs too much" is to ask "How far apart are we?" or "How much is too much?" Simple questions such as these will determine what they think your product should cost.

When you know what they are willing to pay versus your actual cost, you are in a position to overcome the objection. Also, given the objection "It costs too much," you can ask, "In comparison to what?" Again if it's a price objection to other availabilities, it is then a matter of presenting the benefits of differentiation over the competition.

14. THE REDUCTION TO THE RIDICULOUS CLOSE
(Cost-Per-Day Close)

There is a world of difference between willingness to pay and ability to pay. Therefore, when you use the "Calculate the Cost-Per-Day Close," it bridges the gap between willingness and ability to pay.

Whether the objections are "It costs too much," "It's more than I want to pay," or "I only have this much money budgeted" this closing method will easily overcome the money objection, if you determine the difference in your price and spread the cost over a period of time.

For example, your product costs $24,000 and the prospect is only willing to pay $21,000. The discrepancy between the prices is only $3,000. They have committed to $21,000. The concern is $3,000, and that is the amount you have to justify.

You simply spread the difference in price over the lifetime of ownership. For example, suppose an automobile has a product life of five years.

Super achiever: *Mr. Prospect, I appreciate your concern and $3,000 seems like a major amount until you break it down. (Hand the prospect your calculator and allow him to work through the math with you.) Let's say, hypothetically, you will own this for five years, does that sound reasonable?*

Prospect: *I suppose I would have it five years.*

Super achiever: *If we divide $3,000 by the five years we get $600 per year, don't we? Now let's divide $600 by 52 weeks per year, and we arrive at $11.54 per week. Isn't that correct? Of course there are seven days per week so would you mind dividing 11.54 by 7? That's only $1.65 per day.*

(Sometimes your prospect will say this is ridiculous, so before the objection surfaces, steal the objection in advance.)

"Mr. Prospect, I know this might seem ridiculous, but if you think about it, that $3,000 really isn't that much when you consider you could own what you really want and deserve for only $1.65 a day. You're not going to let $1.65 per day stand in the way, are you?"

A real pro performed this technique with a friend several years ago when he was purchasing a wristwatch. He truly wanted to buy a watch that was $650 more than he had budgeted.

This phenomenal salesperson, calculator in hand, said, "Mitch, a nice watch will last a lifetime, but for discussion's sake let's say you only enjoy the watch five years. That's only $130 per year, or $2.50 per week. If we really break it down, it would only be .36 cents per day to own the watch you want rather than having to settle for something else."

15. OBLIQUE COMPARISON CLOSE

From this point she bridged to the oblique comparison close. This is when you compare the difference in price with something that seems inconsequential or minuscule. In this case, she used a soft drink as the oblique comparison.

"Mitch, I bet you probably spend more than .36 cents a day on soft drinks and coffee, don't you? For less than .36 cents, you could own what you deserve. By the way, will that be a personal check or charge?"

16. THE MONEY CLOSE

If you are involved with any product or service where financial terms are offered, here is the procedure you can use every time to break the terms into component parts:

1. **Total Investment** $_____

2. **Initial Investment** $_____

3. **Monthly Investment** $_____

Whenever a prospect says, "I need to think it over," in most cases the main concern is the money. Review the I Want To Think About It Close, on page 94, chapter 9.

Super achiever: *Mr. Prospect, I sense your hesitancy, do you mind my asking is it the money?*

Prospect: *Well, actually it is a little more than we anticipated.*

(Note: By breaking the money into component parts, you will determine if it is the total investment, monthly investment or initial investment that is blocking the sale).

Super achiever: *I can certainly understand, so why don't we take a look at the total offering.*

1. **Total Investment:** $_____

   Do you feel comfortable with the value?

2. **Initial Investment:** $_____

   Is that amount comfortable, or do you
   have that readily available?

3. **Monthly Investment:** $_____

   How does that work with your budget?

Suppose, after running through this scenario, he is comfortable with the total investment and initial investment, but the monthly investment is the challenge. You may then be in a position to offer terms. "I can understand Mr. Prospect, but just suppose I could offer longer terms from three to five years and reduce the monthly investment by $97. Does that place it within your budget?"

What if he says it's the initial investment? (Which, by the way, my father always told me, if it were not for the down payment, a salesperson could sell anything, because society today is only concerned with "How much per month?") You can say: "I understand Mr. Prospect, the initial investment is a little more than anticipated. You tell me how far apart we are. I'm working for you."

Of course, if he is comfortable with the monthly investment and the initial investment, the total investment objection (price) can be overcome by showing value or using the Cost-Per-Day Close.

Just remember, when prospects hesitate with the price, and there are terms offered, it may not be the cost that places it out of reach. Your stumbling block could be in one of the components of the cost which is total investment, monthly investment or initial investment.

Additional Price Responses

1. Your price is too high:

> In comparison to what?
> How much did you think it would cost?
> How high is too high?

2. You've got to do better than that:

> What do you mean better?
> How far apart are we?
> Are you saying you are prepared to make an offer?

3. It costs too much:

> Today most things do.
> How much do you feel it should cost?

4. I can get it for less from your competitor:

> I can appreciate that Mr. Prospect,
> that being the case why haven't
> you purchased from them yet?

Note: That's a bold response, but he will tell you what's keeping him buying from the competition.

5. How much is it?

> That's the best part. Could we come back
> to that in just a moment?

11

Advanced Closing Skills: Urgency and the Take Away

The salesperson's greatest enemies are prospects' indecision and procrastination. It is common for customers to want to procrastinate, and most people will delay making a buying decision if they feel they can benefit by holding off. As a matter of fact, most prospects will delay the decision even though they know it's exactly what they want or need.

How do you overcome indecision and procrastination? *Urgency.* You lead your prospect to take action today by igniting a fire that creates a sense of urgency which provokes and excites your prospect to buy **now** before it's too late.

"Too late" means the conditions surrounding the offer will be different at a later date if the prospect decides to procrastinate. Too late means the circumstances will not only change, but they may also have an adverse effect on the buyer if he delays the decision to own.

You may say there is a limited availabilty, and what you are offering may not be obtainable at a later date. Or, perhaps there is an impending price increase, and the product or service will soon cost more. Whatever the situation, whether availabilty or price, the conditions for buying will not be as favorable as they are right now. This urgency is what compels a prospect to buy *now*.

The Fear of Loss and Desire for Gain

Your prospects' and customers' two greatest buying motivations are the fear of loss and the desire for gain. Fear of loss causes people to feel they will miss out or lose if they don't own something. Also, people love what they cannot have, and as a matter of fact, most people do not even realize how badly they want to own until it is suggested to them that they cannot have it.

Whereas, the desire for gain is based on how the prospect perceives his satisfaction as a result of owning your product or service. The prospect is not so much buying a product as he is aquiring the perceived feelings of satisfaction or dream fulfillment that can only be realized by ownership.

You are always selling to the prospect's emotions. The emotion of fear or the emotion of satisfaction will determine whether your prospect purchases or not. Therefore, the top salespeople are those who incorporate the desire for gain with the fear of loss in their sales presentations.

Urgency Surrounds You

Advertisers and marketers bombard us with urgency and the fear of loss everywhere we turn. "Year end close-out," "Inventory reduction," "We're overstocked and must make way for the new," "Bankruptcy and foreclosure sale," are excellent reasons for the consumer to act immediately.

An automobile salesperson tells his customer, "We have just had a price increase, but I do have just this one at the price I quoted. Let's go ahead and secure this right now, because there is someone else who wants it too."

Timing, Limited Offer, One of a Kind

Timing: Urgency is always planned with an impending event in mind and this is referred to as the impending-event close.

Retailers say, "I'm expecting a price increase any day now." With the impending event, the prospect's timing is everything and the longer he waits the more it may cost. In all cases, the impending event causes the prospect to buy now or suffer the consequences of higher prices later.

Limited Offer. Limited offers are given with a deadline about to occur and the items for sale are restricted to a definite time frame. Limited offers could be a simple Columbus Day special only, or a sale that is offered through the end of the month.

Vacation-ownership resorts utilize the limited offer by structuring the entire product around a time frame. Guests are invited for a complimentary weekend and marketers and sales professionals alike realize if the decision to own is not obtained on the day of the visit, they will never see the prospect again. Therefore they create a list of benefits and incentives that are available only on the day of visit. This is not to say the prospect cannot come back and purchase anytime he desires. It's just that on the day of the presentation, incentives are so attractive, it's in the interest of the prospect to take advantage of the offering.

One of a Kind

Of course the most common, yet powerful, form of urgency is the "One of a kind." It is a popular method and is used when a person is hesitating and cannot seem to make up his mind. The salesperson suddenly halts the presentation and says, "I may have gotten ahead of myself. Before we go any further, let me make sure we even have what you are looking for in stock." And the salesperson returns and says, "Great news, I have *one* left." The prospect cannot believe it nor can the salesperson. Suddenly the prospect is compelled to an instantaneous decision to purchase.

Selling From Strength

With urgency, it is important to sell from a position of strength and appear indifferent about whether the prospect buys or not. In our teenage years we called this playing hard to get with respect to getting dates. Selling from strength uses the element of reverse psychology that makes people want something they may not be able to get. In other words you create a need (desire for gain) and then indicate it may be hard to fulfill (fear of loss).

17. THE TAKE AWAY CLOSE

This is the close for those who have mastered sales basics. You must possess and convey an "I don't care" attitude and be able to sell from strength. The point is, you really do not care if the prospect becomes involved, because regardless if she chooses to own or not, someone else is waiting for the opportunity to buy from you.

This close is based on the "fear of loss." You have been encouraging a "desire for gain" by giving a brilliant presentation, but the prospects may be hesitating and still have not made up their minds. So rather than continue to speak in terms of what the prospects gain, you shift gears. Now you will speak in terms of what the prospects will lose by not taking action:

> **Super achiever:** *Mr. & Mrs. Prospect, I can see you are absolutely enthralled with this gorgeous homesite. But since you are unable to make up your mind, I have a suggestion that will help you avoid disappointment. As you are aware, this is the only homesite at this price. In the event someone else decides to purchase **your** homesite before you do, why don't we go and select another one "almost as nice." (The critical instruction:* **Remain perfectly silent.**)

> **Prospects:** *We don't want a homesite "almost as nice." Besides everything else is more expensive.*

Move into your closing sequence and assumptively conclude the transaction with the Order Form Close. (People do not know how badly they want something until you suggest they cannot have it.)

Review of the "One of A Kind" close:

Super achiever: *Before we go any further, let me call my office and be sure I even have this item in stock. Would that be OK?*

Prospect: *Yes, sure. See if it's available.*

(Note: If you are given permission to check availabilities the prospect has decided to own.)

Super achiever: *I'm glad I called; we are in luck. There was just one left at the warehouse.*

(Note: Move into an Assumptive Close and conclude the sale.)

Urgency-Building Statements

1. There is only one left.

2. There are several salespeople showing the same thing.

3. This is a limited promotion and I'm unable to extend the price we offer today.

4. Someone else is looking at the very same item.

5. Rather than let this slip away, why don't we put this on "temporary hold" while we go back out for a test drive.

12

The Best of the Rest

Additional Powerhouse Closing Strategies

A fter you have mastered overcoming objections found in chapter 6 and "The Baker's Dozen" power techniques in chapter 9, it's time to build up additional closing strategies. The world's highest paid sales professionals are those who are constantly practicing and building their closing techniques. Rest assured, your thorough knowledge of these multiple techniques will not only improve your results, but also build your self-confidence and income.

18. MY LAWYER OR ACCOUNTANT CLOSE

We have all had a prospect tell us our offer seemed to be the perfect solution, **but. . .** before making a final decision he says, "I need to run this by my lawyer or accountant."

When a prospect says he needs a third-party approval, either he is using a smoke-screen objection or he is controlled by his fears.

If however, obtaining advice from a third party, such as a lawyer, accountant or financial advisor is a valid objection, recognize the prospect's fears. When the prospect says, "I cannot make a decision without seeking the approval of an outside advisor," he simply needs someone to assure him it's a wise decision.

The Lawyer or Accountant Close incorporates the closing strategy of "subject to" or "conditional-terms" selling:

A

Prospect: *This seems to be the perfect solution **but**, before making my final decision, I need to run this by my lawyer (or accountant).*

Super achiever: *I can understand. Then am I correct in assuming you are totally satisfied, and there is no question in your mind that you feel it's the right thing for you to do?*

Prospect: *Yes, I'm satisfied. I just want her to look it over.*

Super achiever: *Great, then the only question is whether your lawyer or accountant says, "It's the right thing to do," is that correct?*

Prospect: *That's it.*

Super achiever: *Mr. Prospect, may I ask you a question? (pause). Just suppose your lawyer were present at this very moment, and she advised you to take advantage of the offering, would you act today?*

Prospect: *I suppose I would.*

Super achiever: *Unfortunately she is not with us today, but prior to your speaking with her and to facilitate the transaction in a timely fashion, let's prepare the paperwork now and we will make the sale "subject to" her final approval. This way, the process has begun and if by chance she doesn't not agree, we will simply start over. That makes perfect sense doesn't it?*

If the prospect agrees to the the paperwork "subject to," you are now involved in the process and you can facilitate the details of the sale with the lawyer, accountant or advisor, answering questions and overcoming the third party's objections personally.

19. THE ERRONEOUS CONCLUSION CLOSE

With this close you intentionally make an erroneous statement about a detail that has been decided upon and confirmed earlier in the sales conversation. When you purposely make the erroneous statement, the prospect will correct you and walk right into the sale.

Here's an example using the delivery date:

Super achiever: *Mr. Prospect, let me make sure I have all details. You require delivery on the 30th of the month. Is that correct?*

Prospect: *No, it must be delivered by the 15th.*

Super achiever: *You're right. I apologize. I see it in my notes.*

By correcting you, the prospect has closed the sale with his own words, and you now assumptively begin concluding the transaction.

20. MAYBE I SHOULD WAIT CLOSE

Sometimes referred to as the "Timing is Not Right Close." This is a perfect method to overcome procrastination or to uncover a smoke-screen objection. There are two ways to address "Maybe I should wait." The first is to answer the question with a question:

A

Prospect: *I'm not sure of the timing, maybe I should wait six months?*

Super achiever: *Maybe you should, Mr. Prospect. May I ask a question though?*

Prospect: *Sure.*

Super achiever: *What will be different six months from now? (Remain silent and listen for the concerns and final objections. It may just be a matter of offering concessions such as terms. Listen carefully and the prospect may reveal something minor you can overcome.)*

B

You may also answer "Maybe I Should Wait" with Zig Ziglar's famous close!

Prospect: *Maybe I Should Wait.*

Super achiever: *"Maybe you should wait. Because anytime you make a decision to invest in something there is always a possibility of loss.*

I know there are a couple of things in my life I probably would have been better off had I waited. I know when my wife and I got married, had we waited we could have had a honeymoon to end all honeymoons. I know when we had our first child it wasn't the right timing. Had we waited a few years we could have given him anything he wanted. And I know if I had waited when I purchased my first home, I could have built a really nice first home. Before you venture out of town, the problem with waiting until all the lights are green is, you just might spend your entire life where you are. If you wait until everything is just right, you will never own anything you are entitled to own and enjoy.

Since you want it, and it will be of benefit to you, can you really think of any reason why you shouldn't treat yourself and your family to what you all deserve? The initial investment is only 10 percent. Will you be using a credit card or check today?

21. ULTIMATUM CLOSE

This is the close where you issue your final proposal. This technique requires confidence and strength with the attitude no one sale will break your career or life.

We have all had the experience where you make multiple calls and presentations to a person or committee and someone says "We'll get back to you," asking for additional information and time to "think about it."

You have invested considerable time, even more so than normal.

The prospect has all the information, yet he can't seem to make a decision, so you issue the ultimatum, the Final Decision Close.

You prepare the contracts in their entirety with the same information you have discussed. Bring the contract to the client and say:

> **Super achiever:** *Mr. Prospect, we have covered every issue and concern. You have an immense amount of time invested and so do I. Either this is a good idea or it is not, and one way or another let's reach a positive outcome right now.*

Take your contract and pen and hand it to the prospect. "If you authorize the agreements, I'll process your order promptly." (Remain perfectly silent.)

Regardless of the outcome, at least you are through chasing phantoms and wasting anymore of your time.

I shared this close with a Fortune 500 Company and they customized the technique to use for their mailing list. It seems they had two lists, one for those who regularly purchased and the other for those who never purchased. Yet, they continued to mail the same brochures and information to the people on both lists.

They applied the Ultimatum Close and designed a letter with a postage-paid response card. The letter in essence said: Through the years we have mailed you information without your response. If you wish to continue receiving brochures and information, please return the postcard, and we will keep you on the list, otherwise this is our last contact.

The response was overwhelming. Most did not reply, but they

saved a fortune in brochures and postage and redirected their savings to new prospects and customers who purchased. They now send this ultimatum mailing annually.

22. MERCEDES CLOSE

People usually want what they can't have or afford, and sometimes if a person is financially unable to own the best, he would rather not own it at all. It's called champagne and caviar taste while on a beer and pretzel budget.

For the prospect who insists on only owning the best regardless of his qualifications, try this:

Super achiever: *Mr. Prospect, recently I invested in a new automobile. It was a brand new Nissan Maxima. Ideally though, I wanted to own a Mercedes Benz. Like yourself, I only want to own the best, yet financially I wasn't ready. It's not that the Mercedes was unaffordable, it just wasn't prudent.*

One day I will drive the Mercedes, yet right now, I'm driving what makes perfect sense and it takes me where I want to go in fine style.

Rather than denying yourself ownership and its benefits, why don't you get started with what's prudent. Later, when it makes perfect sense, you can take the equity in your investment and put it toward what you ideally want when you are in a new position. Mr. Prospect for only 10 percent I can schedule delivery on the 1st or the 10th? What works best for you?

23. I'M STILL SHOPPING CLOSE

The "I'm Still Shopping Close" is used when a person or company owner says he wants to compare your price and offer with the competition before making a decision. In some cases this is an unavoidable objection and there are those who simply enjoy the process of shopping and negotiating.

The key to this close is you must give a sound reason why he should not go through the agony of going door to door or salesperson to salesperson trying to find a better price.

The following technique is especially effective if you have been in business for several years or can substantiate the fact your company dominates the market share.

A

Prospect: *Before I make the final decision, I would like to shop around to be sure I'm getting the best possible price.*

Super achiever: *Mr. Prospect, I can certainly appreciate you wanting to shop for the best possible value. That's just smart business, and I would like to make you aware we have been in business for 12 years and have helped many people just like yourself. As a matter of fact, most of our business is repeat customers and referrals who through the years shopped our (product, services, prices) before they made their final decision and invested with our company. Why put yourself through the agony of trying to locate a better value, when the shopping has already been performed for you by smart shoppers* *just like yourself? Let's go ahead and wrap up the details now.*

B

Another method to combat "I'm shopping around" is to offer an incentive or a "today only special." Years ago my wife and I were shopping for a dining room suite. We lived approximately 75 miles from the nearest metropolitan area and had dedicated the entire day to shopping for the best value. We entered our first store early in the morning and found what we considered the perfect dining room suite at a great price, and it was on sale. But, this was our first showroom, so naturally we decided to shop around to assure ourselves we were not making a hasty decision.

The salesperson, knowing we were about to depart, brought in her manager who produced a written warranty that guaranteed if we were to find the same dining room suite at a better price they would not only refund the difference, they would give us 10 percent off the purchase price.

This guarantee reduced our fears, and they closed the sale with urgency. "Mr. and Mrs. Barnes not only do we guarantee the best value, but as you know this suite is on sale, and it is the 'only one' we have. Are you willing to risk someone else purchasing your dining room while you shop around?"

We acquired that dining room suite 13 years ago, and last year we gave it to a young couple who are now receiving as much pleasure as we did when we purchased it. That sales manager performed a great service, and we spent the rest of the day having fun rather than using an entire day shopping for furniture.

Whenever you can offer a guarantee or an incentive, you increase the likelihood of concluding the sale for the person who is shopping. A strong incentive, such as inclusion of a value-added benefit if your prospect purchases today, will make the difference.

C

The final strategy to combat shopping around is what is called "The Always Be Last Close." When you are absolutely convinced your prospect will be shopping, always be last.

With this close never argue, but congenially issue the invitation to shop.

> **Super achiever:** *Mr. Prospect, I understand you need to check other availabilities and prices. However, before you go shopping, I was wondering, you are not the type of person who makes instantaneous buying decisions, are you?*

> **Prospect:** *No. That's why I want to shop.*

> **Super achiever:** *Great, then will you promise me something, and that is before you make your final decision, come back to see me, and I promise you will receive the best value possible.*

> **Prospect:** *Sure, I'll not make the final decision without checking with you first.*

Now, there's a chance the prospect is subconsciously committed to see you last. The idea that you may be able to offer a better value will entice the prospect back to you before rendering a final decision.

In some cases, the prospect will say, "Why don't you just give me your best price now?" Resist the temptation to give in or you may never see the prospect again, because it's possible he will use your final price to negotiate with the competition. Simply tell the prospect:

> **Super achiever:** *Go out and get the best price you can and then come back and see me. I'm certain, when all is said and done, I'll be the one to give you the very best value.*

When the prospect does come back to see if you can beat the best price he received, by all means be ready to do it if possible. If you can not beat the price, explain it's because you have the best value, which includes warranty, delivery, setup and a host of other value-added services.

> **Super achiever:** *You're right, it is a higher price but look what you receive. It includes the warranty, delivery and free installation today. Mr. Prospect, you do want to begin enjoying the benefits today, don't you?*

24. THE SUMMARY CLOSE

As you approach the end of your presentation, the prospect is faced with the task of having to arrange all of your information into a clear and concise picture before she is able to render a decision.

As I stated before, you are always selling benefits, and you summarize them in a manner which proves your product meets her needs. This will raise her buying temperature just before you ask for the order.

Here is a 4-step process to develop your summary close:

Step 1—Bridge into your Summary Close with a transition statement:

Ms. Prospect, we have covered a lot of territory today! Before moving forward, let's review the highlights of our discussion.

Step 2—Reconfirm your prospect's wants, needs and desires:

You mentioned your plan would have to provide for your company's immediate results. Is that correct?

Your primary concern is increased sales and higher productivity. Is that on target?

And of course, because of prior budget commitments, ideally, you would prefer monthly or quarterly billing? Have I included every-thing?

Step 3—Summarize how your product or service meets the prospect's wants, needs and desires:

For immediate results and convenience, we will provide a 3-day on-site sales education program to acquaint and teach your team the basics of sales. From here we will meet once weekly for a 2-hour class to reinforce sales education, as well as customize a sales pres-entation for your people to sell your product/service.

Concerning increased sales and productivity, based on past experi-ences with companies similar to yours, you should experience a 20 percent increase in sales. In many cases increases are even greater.

Now, the best part of this proposal is the terms. With a small initial *investment of $_____ the balance will be due in monthly investments of $_____, just as you have requested.*

Step 4—Ask for the order and close the sale: (Tie Down Close)

Wouldn't you agree our services exceed your initial expectations? This program pays for itself, as well as provides you with the results and profits you seek, am I correct? I have taken the liberty to prepare the paperwork. All that's necessary is your authorization.

A common question aspiring super achievers ask is how to actually transition to the final closing sequence. The Summary Close is the perfect method to "bridge" into your final close. You summarize the benefits, even if there are as many as 20 or more items and say: "When would you like to get started?" "Why don't you give it a try," or "The initial investment is 10 percent, would that be cash or check?" If acceptance is gained you simply conclude the sale with the Order Form Close. If an objection is offered, you identify and overcome the final objection, thus closing the sale.

25. PAINT A FANTASY PICTURE CLOSE

We are all sensitive and receptive to the suggestive influences of the people around us. In sales this has particular significance because it means when you are excited, your excitement and enthusiasm are contagious and will be transferred to the buyer. (We discussed this at the beginning of the book.)

The Paint A Fantasy Picture Close also piggy-backs on the Assumptive Close in that you speak to the prospects in terms as if they already own your product or service. Your enthusiastic suggestions will actually paint vivid mental pictures of what it is going to be like to use and enjoy your product or service.

Once a salesperson used this type of close when a friend of mine was shopping for a new automobile. Andy was intent on owning a special sports car. He had narrowed his choice between a Trans Am, or an Iroc-Z Camero. In Andy's estimation either was the car of his choice and he was going to purchase as most buyers do, on the basis of price.

He entered the Trans Am dealership and met a less than enthusiastic salesperson who proceeded to tell him he had "the best deals." He told Andy he was proud of the amount of "steel" and "number of units" he pushed every month. To be frank, he offered a good price, but Andy was somewhat dismayed. After all, this was a sports car, a dream machine, not a unit or a piece of steel.

He asked the salesperson's best price, as all shoppers do, and then visited the Camero dealership. Here he met a salesperson who epitomized excitement and enthusiasm. When Andy mentioned he was interested in an Iroc-Z Camero, the salesperson asked a brilliant question.

"Andy, can you afford the tickets?" Andy looked at him bewildered, and the salesperson followed up with another incredible question. "Do you know how fast an Iroc-Z is capable of going? Andy, I have great values on the Iroc-Z so price will not be a concern today. You just have to think about affording the tickets you could get for speeding with the speed this car is capable of reaching."

"Andy, do you have a girlfriend or wife?"

"Well yes, I'm married."

"Andy, you don't think your wife is going to allow you to cruise around town in this machine without her, do you? You're going to love the way the Iroc handles, and before you test drive your new car, let's remove the 'T-Tops.'"

It's probably unnecessary to say Andy drove home in the Iroc without the 'T-Tops,' but not before swinging by the beach without his wife. It is important, however to mention how Andy purchased his car. The Iroc was more expensive than the Trans AM's best price, which proves a customer's consideration is not only getting the best deal. The Trans AM's salesperson suggested the emotional payoff of steel and units at a good deal. The Iroc's value was power, prestige and dream fulfillment, conveyed by an excited salesperson who suggestively appealed to Andy's emotions before he ever took ownership.

With the Paint A Fantasy Close, you enthusiastically create mental images in the mind of your prospects of what it's going to be like to use, benefit and enjoy your product or service. With this close, your suggestions move them immediately into the mindset of how they will enjoy owning.

Examples of Paint a Fantasy

1. Mr. & Mrs. Prospect, your children and grandchildren will love spending summer days with you around your new pool.

2. Close your eyes. . . picture yourself relaxing on the beach, enjoying the sun during the day and then capping the evening off with a view of a romantic sunset. That's the vacation you really want, isn't it?

3. Can't you just smell the steaks on the grill as you enjoy weekends at your very own mountain retreat?

26. LOST SALE CLOSE

Sometimes referred to as the Door Knob Close, this is used as the final close. You have delivered your presentation, utilized your best closing strategies, yet it seems hopeless that the prospect will make a decision. Begin this close by packing up your paperwork and thanking him for his time. Act like you realize the situation is hopeless and you are giving up. When the prospect thinks you are going to leave, his buying resistance drops because he thinks the presentation is over.

While you are seated with your packed briefcase, or standing ready to reach for the door knob say:

Super achiever: *Mr. Prospect, I realize you are not going to own today, but I wonder if you could help me with my presentation. Could you share with me the reason why you are not going to become involved today? I don't want to make the same mistake again that I have made with you. What's the real reason for not owning today?*

Remain perfectly silent and listen carefully for his real reason as well as for hot buttons you may have missed. Now, the prospect relieved of tension, will in most cases, tell you the hidden concern or reason why he is not going to purchase. After obtaining the real reason (final objection) sit back down and say:

> **Super achiever:** *Mr. Prospect, thank you. I'm so glad you brought that to my attention. Obviously, I did not explain that portion of the offering very well. May I make an attempt to explain that one more time? (Start your presentation over.)*

Most salespeople, out of fear, will not go the extra mile with this final closing attempt. But I can attest that it has worked for me. I have retrieved at least a dozen seemingly lost sales from qualified customers who would not reveal their hidden reason for moving forward until I used this final closing method.

A Closing Thought

Every profession in the world has its own failure rate. Yet sales is the only profession in the world where the standard, normal rate of failure can be 80 to 90 percent. In the best of times, four out of five calls will end in *No*. And in tough economies, when the competition is vicious, the rate is even greater.

In my estimation the difference between failure and success is perception. Your perception will always be your reality. Therefore, do not perceive "failure" as failure, but as a necessary learning experience that must occur for you to achieve success. The super achiever perceives failures as an opportunity to learn and grow and she continues to move forward.

If you become discouraged remember:

✦ Cy Young, baseball's most coveted pitcher, only won 511 games of the 906 he pitched.

✦ Babe Ruth, before achieving the home-run record, first held the record for strikeouts.

✦ Michael Jordan, the celebrated basketball superstar, was cut from his high school team for one year.

✦ Thomas Edison failed 10,000 times before he succeeded in creating the incandescent light.

✦ Colonel Sanders of Kentucky Fried Chicken was retired and over 60-years-old before he decided to make his recipe known. He made close to 1,000 calls and spent nights in his car before he made his first sale.

It is critical to understand as you attempt to master the many closing techniques, you still risk failure. And so it is while attempting anything new. I will assure you it's all right to fail when first trying the closing techniques, but it's not all right to avoid learning and mastering the techniques. Failure is not your enemy. Complacency and lack of initiative are your enemies. Rest assured you cannot fail if you do not try. But if you do not try, then by default, you have already failed.

Realize your success will come as you improve by practice, learning, memorizing and internalizing proven principles.

Take these proven principles, techniques, methods and strategies and persist. And if you will persist, I promise you will achieve the success you want and so richly deserve.

Life is queer with its twists and turns,

As everyone of us sometimes learns,

And many a failure turns about,

When he might have won had he stuck it out,

Don't give up though the race seems slow,

You may succeed with another blow.

Success is failure turned inside out.

The silver tint of the clouds of doubt,

And you can never tell how close you are,

It may be near when it seems so far,

So stick to the fight when you're hardest hit,

It's when things seem worse,

That you must not quit.

Author, unknown

13

$\mathbf{R}$ecap—
$\mathbf{C}$ommon $\mathbf{O}$bjections
and $\mathbf{E}$ffective
$\mathbf{R}$esponses

A

Will you discount (cut) your commission?

a. Super achiever: *I can appreciate why you're asking, and I'll be up front with you and say no. I will not adjust my fees for this reason. As a professional, my time has a certain value and I only work with people like yourself, who realize the value of professional service.*

b. Super achiever: *Please do not think of what I earn as a commission. My earnings are based on a fee for service, and I can promise you my service will far outweigh the fee.*

163

Will you adjust your commission? Your competition will.

Super achiever: *You're right Mr. Prospect, there are a lot of desperate representatives out there and I'm concerned. May I share why?*

We are talking about a person who doesn't even see the value in himself, and if he doesn't value himself do you think he will value your business?

B

Will you "adjust the price" or "discount the listed price?"

a. Super achiever: *Why do you ask, are you considering owning?*

b. Super achiever: *I'm curious if you are familiar with how a product or service's true value is determined. In reality, value is not determined by what the manufacturer or those who represent the product feel it should cost. Value is based on comparable sales. In other words, a product or service is only worth the last price that it was purchased for. If yesterday someone purchased it at $100 and today you buy it for $90, but tomorrow someone negotiates to $80, then what is the true value? Mr. Prospect, we offer value protection and feel everyone should obtain the same fair price, don't you?*

c. Super achiever: *We do not negotiate. Our products are very beneficial. We think everyone should receive the same great value. After all that's what's really important, isn't it?*

d. Super achiever: *Many years ago, our company made a fundamental decision—to justify price once, rather than apologize for poor quality an entire lifetime. If price is your only concern, obviously I must not have presented the true value. If I may, let's review the features and benefits of owning, and then we can further discuss our value-added services, such as extended warranties, installation and delivery, as well as the host of additional services offered.*

C

I did not bring my checkbook.

a. Super achiever: *That's fine, but you say you would like to own and are prepared to proceed forward, except you do not have your checkbook?*

(Note: It is important you ask the question, to confirm if the checkbook is the only reason prohibiting ownership.)

Prospect: *Yes.*

Super achiever: *I understand, and so we can go ahead today and start the paperwork, any denomination of cash will serve as a good-faith deposit and place a hold on this product or service you desire. What amount do you have available today?*

I did not bring my checkbook and I don't have cash.

a. Super achiever: *That's fine, but you are saying you would like to own and are prepared to proceed forward, except you do not have your checkbook or cash available?*

Prospect: *Yes.*

Super achiever: *That's fine, I understand. We won't let these reasons prohibit ownership. Let's go ahead and prepare the paperwork, and then I'll place your item on hold. Tomorrow morning I'll drop by, or you can deliver a check to our office. What would be most* *convenient for you? Should I drop by or do you want to come to the office?*

D

I have a good friend in the business.

a. Super achiever: *I can appreciate that, so I can understand your frustration of feeling obligated to do business with your friend. Yet, from a friendship perspective, you owe your friend your friendship. From a business perspective, you owe yourself the best. You do want the best working for you, don't you?*

Prospect: *Yes.*

Super achiever: *Your friend will want the very best for you too, won't he?*

E

Why should I choose you or your company?

The only way to answer this objection is for you to take the time to identify your strengths and differentiate yourself from the competition. I leave this one up to you. However, most consumers see a salesperson as a commodity. They feel we're all alike—one is the same as the other.

If you have not identified why a customer would choose you, then certainly the customer will be unable to understand why he should choose you too.

F

I'll buy used.

a. Super achiever: Are you willing to take that kind of risk?

b. **Super achiever:** *Have you ever bought anything of this type before? In most cases, used equipment is only available because the original owner has no use for it any more. Are you willing to sacrifice the peace of mind that accompanies factory warranties and guarantees?*

G

I'm just looking.

a. **Super achiever:** *Looking at a new (product) is fun, isn't it?*

Prospect: Yes, it is.

Super achiever: *Have you had an opportunity to look at other (products), or have you had the opportunity to look elsewhere?*

Prospect: *Yes.*

Super achiever: *Great, what have you "looked at" that you like?*

Prospect: *No I haven't "looked" elsewhere or at anything else.*

Super achiever: *Outstanding, you have come to the right place.*

(Note: You may conclude the process with the I'm Still Shopping Close.)

H

Getting past the gatekeeper (secretary).

    a. Super achiever: *Who am I speaking to please? Thank you (person's name.) My name is_____ .Please connect me with _____.*

    b. Super achiever: *Hello, my name is____. It is important I speak to_____. Would you please connect us?*

    c. Super achiever: *I understand your employer is busy, and so am I. That's why I'm calling. I'll be out of the office and impossible to reach. Please connect us.*

I

I'm too busy to talk.

    a. Super achiever: *I can appreciate that, time truly is our most precious resource, isn't it? Since we both are busy and have a mutual respect for our time, I promise to be brief.*

    b. Super achiever: *I appreciate you are busy. That's exactly why I'm calling you. I find those who are busiest are my best customers because they have a true need for our products and services. May I explain why to you?*

J

We've been doing business with the same company for years.

    a. Super achiever: *Thank you. I think loyalty is a virtue, and out of respect for your loyalty, I'm not asking you to give up your relationship. What's more, I'll not ask for all your business, I only ask for a small portion. And from here, I'll earn any additional business. Why don't you give it a try?*

b. **Super achiever:** *I respect your loyalty and the many years of your business relationship. I can assure you the vast majority of my customers are just as loyal, would you like to know why?*

K

I need to run this by my boss or the committee.

(Note: As stated earlier, in most cases this objection is caused by lack of proper qualification.)

a. **Super achiever:** *I understand, and you will recommend they go forward with this proposal, won't you?* (Note: This question confirms his or her true position.)

b. **Super achiever:** *When do you meet? Great, I'll adjust my schedule and be there to deliver the presentation with you.*

c. **Super achiever:** *I understand. What will you discuss with them? And of course, mine is the recommendation you will make, isn't it?*

L

I'm not interested.

a. **Super achiever:** *Of course you are not. How could you be interested without knowing anything about the benefits?*

b. **Super achiever:** *Mr. Prospect, I promise I'm not going to try to sell you anything. I'm only here to present to you the reasons why so many others like yourself, who initially were not interested, decided to take advantage of our offer. If what I share with you does not agree with your philosophy or budget, then I will understand. You be the judge. Is that fair?*

M

It's not a good time, my business is off.

a. **Super achiever:** *I understand. Perhaps my service will be the answer.*

b. **Super achiever:** *Just because business is off, does not mean you should slow down. Now's the time to dig in. I'm glad I'm here. Let's you and I take proactive measures to insure this will not happen again.*

N

I don't have a budget at this time.

a. **Super achiever:** *That's why I'm here. The increased productivity and results you will experience will make the cost of ownership almost free.*

b. **Super achiever:** *When would the next budget allocation be? Great, why don't we meet now, and we will have everything in place when the funds are allocated.*

c. **Super achiever:** *I can certainly appreciate that. That's exactly why our best customers choose to own with the benefit of our financial arrangements. Are you aware we offer terms?*

Bibliography
and Recommended
Resources

This bibliography contains the majority of research and resources used in writing this book. I highly recommend you include the following titles in your personal success library.

Advanced Selling Strategies, Brian Tracy, Simon and Schuster, Inc., 1995

How to Master the Art of Selling, Tom Hopkins, Warner Books, 1982

The Official Handbook For New Home Salespeople, Bob Schultz, New Home Specialist, 1989

The Sales Closing Book, Gerhard Gschwandtner, Personal Selling Power, 1988

The Sales Script Book, Gerhard Gschwandtner & Donald J. Moine, Ph.D., Personal Selling Power, 1986

Secrets of Closing the Sale, Zig Ziglar, Fleming H. Revell Company, 1984

Ziglar on Selling, Zig Ziglar, Ballentine Books, 1991

Video Cassettes

Handling Objections, Jack and Jerry Kinder, Nightingale Conant

How to Become a Real Estate Superstar, Mike Ferry, Mike Ferry Productions

How to Become a Super Seller, D. Forbes Ley, Sales Success Institute

The Psychology of Selling, Brian Tracy, Peak Performance Training

38 Proven Ways to Close that Sale, Mark Victor Hansen, Career Trac Publications

24 Techniques for Closing the Sale, Brian Tracy, Nightingale Conant

Audio Cassettes

The Foundations of Modern Selling, J. Douglass Edwards, Tom Hopkins International

The Psychology of Selling, Brian Tracy, Nightingale Conant

Hardball, Robert L. Shook, Nightingale Conant

For Your Continuing Education

Collaborative Selling, Dr. Tony Alessandra and Rick Berrera, John Wiley & Sons, Inc.

Follow-Up: Turn Contacts into Contracts, Myers Barnes, (919) 261-7611

Greatest Salesman in the World, The, Og Mandino, Bantam Books

Franklin Day Planner, Franklin Quest Company, Salt Lake City, Utah

How I Raised Myself From Failure to Success, Frank Bettger, Prentice Hall

How to Market Through Direct Mail, Nido Qubein, Nightingale Conant

Instant Influence, Robert Caildini, Dartnell

Non-Manipulative Selling, Tony Alessandra, Phil Wexler and Rick Barrera, Prentice Hall Press

Platinum Rule, The, Art Fettig, Growth Unlimited

Psychology of Winning, The, Denis Waitley, Nightingale Conant

Relationship Selling, Jim Cathcart, Perigee Books

Sales Bible, The, Jeffrey H. Gitomer, Nightingale Conant

Secrets of Power Negotiating, The, Roger Dawson, Nightingale Conant

Selling Power, Published monthly by Gerhard Gschwandtner. P.O. Box 5467, Fredericksburg, VA 22403. Subscription information, (540) 752-7000

Spin Selling, Neil Rackman, McGraw Hill

Success Is An Inside Job, Lee Milter, Hampton Roads

Index

About the Author

Myers Barnes is president of Myers Barnes Associates, a consulting and sales coaching firm located in Kitty Hawk, North Carolina. Myers is driven by a passion for excellence and positive results. His dynamic presentation style has made him a highly sought-after speaker in the fields of human potential and sales achievement.

The author understands first hand the challenges that face all salespeople, having spent his beginning years as a top-producing sales representative. Later, his career as sales manager and vice president of sales won much acclaim. His practical, yet powerful approach to management and sales coaching strategies has generated millions of dollars in revenues for both individuals and corporations.

In addition to *Closing Strong*, Myers is also the author of *Video Training Follow-up*. He firmly believes the most successful individuals and organizations are those who are constantly enhancing their communication, management and selling skills through training, and he welcomes the opportunity to show you how to reach your own extraordinary potential.

❖ ❖ ❖

If you have questions pertaining to your sales career, please write or call, and Myers will respond personally. For company or group consulting services, training programs, seminars or corporate presentations, please write, call or fax:

Myers Barnes Associates
P.O. Box 50, Kitty Hawk
N.C. 27949
PHONE (252) 261-7611, FAX (252) 261-7615